GNOSTICISM

AMS PRESS

NEW YORK

GNOSTICISM

*a source book of heretical writings
from the early Christian period*

edited by ROBERT M. GRANT

HARPER & BROTHERS
NEW YORK

Library of Congress Cataloging in Publication Data

Grant, Robert McQueen, 1917- ed.
   Gnosticism.

       Reprint of the ed. published by Harper, New York.
       Bibliography: p.
       Includes index.
       1. Gnosticism—History—Sources. I. Title.
   [BT1390.G7   1978]   273'.1   77-85274
   ISBN 0-404-16108-1

273.1
G533

79060414

Reprinted by arrangement with Harper & Row,
Publishers, Inc., from the edition of 1961,
New York.

First AMS edition published in 1978.

MANUFACTURED IN THE UNITED STATES OF AMERICA

This Gnostic anthology was originally prepared for a series, now terminated, published under the auspices of the Committee on the History of Religion of the American Council of Learned Societies. Along the way it has received the benefit of a good deal of revision, especially by A. D. Nock, E. R. Hardy, and W. R. Schoedel. As they now stand, the translations from Greek and Latin documents were made by the editor (except for Corpus Hermeticum I, IV, and VII, originally prepared by F. C. Grant, and XIII, prepared by W. R. Schoedel). The Syriac *Hymn of the Soul*, originally translated by A. A. Bevan in 1897, has been revised by W. R. Schoedel. The translations of the *Gospel of Mary* and *The Secret Book of John* are based on the German version of W. Till as revised from the Coptic by E. R. Hardy. The new translation of the *Gospel of Truth* was made by W. W. Isenberg and was awarded a prize by the Christian Research Foundation.

The translations of biblical passages are not derived from English versions but from the quotations made by Gnostic writers, though references to the Psalms are given in accordance with the English numbering.

I am deeply grateful to Professor Hans Jonas for his reading the manuscript at an early stage, for correcting many of my errors, and for leading me to revise the entire work. Through an oversight this acknowledgement was omitted from the British edition of the book.

Contents

INTRODUCTION

Introduction

The nature and significance of Gnosticism has been a matter of controversy from the first century of our era to the present day. When we look for definitions in a dictionary of recent date, we find " gnosis " described as " a knowledge of spiritual things; mystical knowledge," and we read that a Gnostic is " a member of any of certain sects among the early Christians who claimed to have superior knowledge of spiritual things, and explained the world as created by powers or agencies arising as emanations from the Godhead."[*] The definition of " gnosis " does not make sufficiently clear the fact that gnostic knowledge was regarded as derived solely from revelation and that this revelation was comprehensible only to those who believed, or " knew," that they were spiritual beings innately capable of receiving it. And the definition of " Gnostic," while it does justice to the historical fact that the first Gnostics we encounter in the literature we possess were related to the Christian movement, does not take into account such Gnostic religions as Manichaeism and Mandaeism. Moreover, the whole question of the origin or origins of Gnosticism is exceedingly obscure. Most of the Gnostics whose writings are included in this anthology could be regarded as members of " sects among the early Christians "; but it is by no means certain that their ideas were primarily, or originally, Christian.

Indeed, if (as is possible if not probable) Gnostic ways of thinking are reflected among the opponents of the apostle Paul at Corinth, in Galatia, and at Colossae, it would appear likely that at least some constitutive elements of the Gnostic

[*] C. L. Barnhart, *The American College Dictionary* (New York, 1947), 517.

movement are pre-Christian, even though the highly developed systems of a Basilides or a Valentinus do not appear until the second century. If we reserve the name " Gnostic " for adherents of such systems, we have to admit that something to be called " proto-Gnostic " or " incipiently Gnostic " or " Gnosticising " was in existence at an earlier date.

The purpose of this volume is to present most of the early Gnostic writings, and fragments of writings, which were known to the early Fathers of the Christian Church or were probably in circulation in the Mediterranean world in the first two centuries after the crucifixion of Jesus. It contains most of the known Gnostic literature which appeared within the Graeco-Roman world and made an impact on this world. Some form or forms of Mandaeism may have been in existence during these early centuries, but the influence of Mandaean thought on early Gnostic teachers is so problematical that the Mandaean literature has been excluded.† In consequence, the picture of Gnosticism here provided is focused more on systems of a semi-philosophical kind and less on poetic expression than would otherwise be the case.

We begin with a description of various Gnostic systems, from Simon Magus to the Cainites, which Irenaeus, bishop of Lyons in the late second century, provides towards the end of his first book *On the Detection and Refutation of Gnosis Falsely So-Called*. Part of this account may be derived from a lost treatise by Justin Martyr, a generation earlier than Irenaeus; other sources of Irenaeus' information include authentic Gnostic documents, as well as his own observations. The next section contains two Gnostic works from a Coptic papyrus of the fifth century. One of them, *The Gospel of Mary*, was apparently composed in the third century; the other, *The Secret Book of John*, was already known to Irenaeus, though in a slightly different version. The third section includes various minor, though significant, documents of the second and third centuries: descriptions of two Ophite diagrams by Celsus and Origen, the book *Baruch* by the Gnostic Justin (together with

† For an analysis of it see Hans Jonas, *The Gnostic Religion* (Boston, 1958).

a later Marcionite narrative apparently based on it), some examples of Naassene exegesis, and the ' Hymn of the Pearl ' from the *Acts of Thomas*.

The next two sections contain the systematic theologies of Basilides and his son Isidore and of Valentinus and some of the leading members of his school. These sections represent the semi-philosophical gnosis against which Irenaeus and Hippolytus directed some of their most vigorous attacks. In the last section we present some of the tractates from the Hermetic writings, which may range from the second century to the fourth, as illustrations of Gnosticising tendencies to be found in religious philosophy. We conclude with some of the criticisms directed towards Gnosticism by the Neoplatonists Plotinus and Porphyry.

What is it which binds all this literature together and makes it possible for us to speak of its authors and devotees as Gnostics? After all, in antiquity the adherents of the Gnostic systems did not usually call themselves " Gnostics," and the Church Fathers spoke of them as members of various sects, often named after their founders. Moreover, the word " gnosis " was used among Christians in speaking of the saving knowledge of Christian faith. But there is one element which binds all the various systems together. This is the doctrine, to a considerable extent shared with Jewish apocalyptic writers of the period, that the world is bad; it is under the control of evil or ignorance or nothingness. It cannot be redeemed; indeed, for some Gnostics the world is the equivalent of hell. Only the divine spark, which somehow is imprisoned in some men, is capable of salvation. It is saved when, by divine grace, it comes to know itself, its origin, and its destiny.

This self-knowledge is expressed in a myth which explains how it was possible for the supremely transcendent God, who is essentially unknown and unknowable, to permit the world to come into existence. This supreme being, who in many systems is called " the Absolute Sovereignty " (*authentia*), could not have been directly responsible for an evil world.

Between the world and God, therefore, the Gnostics postulated the existence of spiritual beings with a history of their own. Out of their sin, negligence and ignorance the world of animate and inanimate nature came into being. In some way, however, the divine spark came down from the Sovereignty above and gave men, or some men, their kinship with God and their potentiality of being restored to him. Corresponding to the original descent of the spark was the later descent of the Redeemer, who removed ignorance and brought self-knowledge to spiritual men who were capable of receiving it. In many Gnostic systems there are three classes of men: the spiritual men who are " by nature " or " by origin " saved; the " psychics " who have a latent capacity for gnosis and need to have the Gnostic gospel set before them; and the " earthly " or " material " men who will never be saved. In Valentinianism, for example, the " psychic " men were regarded as primarily consisting of the members of the Catholic Church, since the Christian gospel as ordinarily preached was viewed as a preparation for true gnosis.

The origins of the Gnostic world-view are (as we have already said) extremely controversial. Generally speaking, there are four widely accepted theories. Gnosticism has been regarded as derived from ancient Oriental religion (Zoroastrian, Mesopotamian, sometimes even Indian), or from " heterodox Judaism " (apocalyptic or " mystical "), or from heterodox Christianity, or from late Hellenistic philosophy (especially incipient Neoplatonism). There are aspects of truth in all these theories, and it is possible that no one of them does justice either to the complexity of the phenomena or to the underlying unity of Gnostic thought. It may be that the uniquely Gnostic expression of estrangement and alienation is not susceptible of historical analysis, or that it owes something to a sense of breakdown, not precisely definable, which may have been common in the time when Gnosticism arose. Traditional text-book analyses of " Hellenism " or " Judaism " do not provide much help in dealing with Gnostic origins, for it is coming to be realised that in the first and second centuries there was a tremendous amount of cultural cross-fertilisation; Gnosticism itself provides a significant witness to the vitality of this process.

Some specific aspects of Gnostic thought reflect the operation of some of the factors we have mentioned. For instance, the popularity of astrology meant that men's minds were often fixed on the great spaces above them, upon the fixed stars and the "wandering" planets, which could be regarded as powers malevolent rather than neutral or good. The word "aeon," originally applied to periods of time (the present evil aeon, the future good aeon), came to be used in reference to the spaces governed by astral spirits or to the astral spirits themselves. Apocalyptic eschatology had expressed a dualism related primarily to time; now in Gnostic thought the dualism was thought of in relation to space as well. The highest aeon was the best. Spirit, from above, was good; flesh and matter, from below, were bad.

Many of the systems express an intense hostility towards "the God of the Jews," and the divine names found in the Old Testament are often applied to the planetary spirits. The reason for this hostility may perhaps be found in the rejection of (apocalyptic?) Judaism by Gnostic teachers;* in the Basilidian system described by Irenaeus (Section I-4) and in the Gnostic *Gospel of Philip* we hear of those who as Gnostics are "no longer Jews." Other features of Gnostic teaching suggest that it was related to apocalyptic Judaism, but it was of course anti-Jewish in the form in which we find it.

The figure of the fallen Sophia, who among some Valentinians bore the semi-Hebrew name Achamoth, may be derived from the "daughter of God" or "mother of the universe" (as Philo calls her); but in Gnosticism she has become the subject of an elaborate mythology, as though she were a mother-goddess like those found in Mesopotamia and the Mediterranean world.

The question of the origin of the Gnostic redeemer is remarkably difficult to answer. In pre-Christian Graeco-

* See my *Gnosticism and Early Christianity* (New York, 1959).

Roman religion there was no redeemer or saviour of a Gnostic type. There were gods who died and rose again, but they did not give saving knowledge to their followers. There were rites, even rites which provided immortality, but there was no theological explanation of the rites like that which we find in Gnosticism. In Oriental religions redeemers somewhat analogous to the Gnostic ones may have existed, but thus far no one has been able to prove that they were known as such before the rise of Gnostic thought. To some extent the Gnostic redeemer is foreshadowed in the mysterious Teacher of Righteousness of the Dead Sea Scrolls, but the interpretation of his meaning at Qumran did not make him more than human. The most obvious explanation of the origin of the Gnostic redeemer is that he was modelled after the Christian conception of Jesus. It seems significant that we know no redeemer before Jesus, while we encounter other redeemers (Simon Magus, Menander) immediately after his time.

The elements we have mentioned seemed to be the most important ones in Gnostic thought. It seems to have arisen out of a mixture of Hellenistic, Jewish, Oriental and Christian factors, combined in an atmosphere of intense otherworldliness and imaginative myth-making. One further factor is not as significant as some of the Church Fathers thought. This is the influence of Greek philosophy. To be sure, some Gnostics were fond of philosophical language; but consideration of their systems as wholes suggests that philosophy provided some of their terminology rather than any basic structure or structures.

Because of the importance of Jewish and Christian elements in Gnosticism, such early Church Fathers as Irenaeus, Clement, Tertullian and Hippolytus regarded it as a supremely dangerous enemy to Christian faith, and they took great pains to describe it as exactly as possible in order to refute its tenets. Their writings remain the most important sources for early Gnostic thought which we possess (with the possible exception of Mandaean writings). In addition, we have a fairly wide range of Gnostic documents in Coptic translations, some discovered in the nineteenth century, others found as recently as 1945, when an Ophite-Sethian library came to light near Nag-Hammadi in Egypt. It included forty-four distinct works on papyrus, bound in thirteen leather volumes. Some of these have recently been published; one of the most important of them is *The Gospel of Truth*, perhaps a Valentinian work of the second century. Obviously a great deal of work remains to be done, though it is unlikely that the picture of Gnosticism we already possess will require a great deal of revision.

PART I

THE OLDEST CHRISTIAN GNOSTIC SYSTEMS

The oldest continuous account of various gnostic systems which we possess is that preserved and edited by Irenaeus, Christian bishop of Lyons in southern France, about the year 180. It is to be found in the first book of his treatise "on the discovery and refutation of gnosis falsely so-called," which is usually cited by the title 'Adversus haereses.'* Irenaeus had begun his work with an extended account of various Valentinian systems (see Part V). In Chapter 22 he turned to the task of tracing the origins of all gnostic doctrines to a single source, the heresy of Simon Magus which he found mentioned, or at least alluded to, in the Acts of the Apostles. It is at least possible that most of his information about these systems was already available in a treatise "against all heresies" written by Justin Martyr about 150 but now lost;† but it seems to be impossible to determine exactly what Irenaeus may have added to his source or sources. Probably, however, we can say that Irenaeus added the description of Simon from the book of Acts ('Adv. haer.' i, 23, 1), and the accounts of Carpocrates (25) and Cerdo (27. 1) may well be his. Certainly he has produced his own descriptions of the Encratites and Tatian (28), of the Sethian-Ophites (29-30) and of the Cainites (31. 1-2).

He begins by arguing that to understand gnostic origins is to understand gnosticism.

***

* The numbers in parentheses in each heading refer to the chapters and or sections in Massuet's edition of Irenaeus.

† Justin may be responsible for the picture of Simon as the first Gnostic (cf. *Apol.* i. 26).

Since the work of discovering and refuting all heretics is diverse and manifold, and we have proposed to refute all of them in relation to the character of their teaching, we have considered it necessary to report first their source and root so that, by knowing their most sublime " depth," you may understand the tree from which such fruits have come down [cf. Matt. 7 : 16-20].

I

Simon Magus (23. 1-4)

(1) For Simon the Samaritan was a magician; Luke, the disciple and follower of the apostles, says of him: " There was a certain man named Simon, who was previously in the city, practising magic and leading the race of the Samaritans astray, saying that he was somebody great; they gave heed to him, from the least to the greatest, saying, ' This is the power of God which is called Great.' But they gave heed to him because for a long time he had tricked them with his magic " [Acts viii. 9-11]. Therefore this Simon, who simulated belief (thinking that the apostles worked their cures by magic, not by the power of God) and supposed that when believers in God were filled with the Holy Spirit by the imposition of hands through the Christ Jesus who was proclaimed by the apostles, this actually took place by a greater magical art (and offered money to the apostles so that he himself might also receive this power of giving the Holy Spirit to whomever he wished), heard these words from Peter: " Your money perish with you, since you thought the gift of God could be obtained with money. You have neither part nor lot in this matter, for your heart is not right before God. I see that you are in the gall of bitterness and the bond of iniquity " [Acts viii. 20-21, 23].

And when he had still more disbelieved in God, he eagerly proceeded to contend against the apostles,* so that he himself

* See p. 27.

might seem to be famous, and he investigated all magic still more carefully so that he could compel the multitude to marvel—since he lived under Claudius Caesar, by whom, it is said, he was honoured with a statue because of his magic.

He was glorified as a god by many, and he taught that he himself was the one who was to appear among the Jews as Son, would descend in Samaria as Father, and would come among the other nations as Holy Spirit.† He said that he was the Absolute Sovereignty, i.e. the Father above all, and was willing to be called whatever men call him.

(2) Simon the Samaritan, from whom all heresies originated, provided his sect with subject-matter of this kind. He led about with him a certain Helen, after he had redeemed her from a life of prostitution in Tyre, a city of Phoenicia. He said she was the first conception of his mind, the Mother of all, through whom in the beginning he had the idea of making angels and archangels. This Thought, leaping forth from him and knowing what her father willed, descended to the lower regions and generated angels and powers, by whom this world was made. But after she generated them, she was held captive by them because of envy, for they did not want to be considered the offspring of anyone else. For Simon was entirely unknown to them; his Thought was held captive by the powers and angels emitted by her. She suffered all kinds of humiliation from them, so that she did not run back upwards to her Father but was even enclosed in a human body, and through the ages transmigrated as from one vessel to another, into other female bodies.

She was in that Helen because of whom the Trojan war was undertaken. Therefore when Stesichorus‡ vilified her in his poems he was deprived of his eyesight; later, when he repented and wrote the *Palinodes*, in which he praised her, his sight was restored.

Transmigrating from body to body, and always enduring humiliation from the body, she finally became a prostitute; she was the " lost sheep " [Luke 15 : 6]. For this reason he

† See p. 28.

came, in order to rescue her first and free her from her bonds, then to offer men salvation through his " knowledge."

For when the angels misgoverned the world, since each of them desired the primacy, he came for the reformation of affairs; he descended,§ transformed and made like the powers and authorities and angels, so that among men he appeared as a man, though he was not a man, and he seemed to suffer in Judaea, though he did not suffer.

The prophets spoke their prophecies under the inspiration of the angels who made the world. Therefore those who have set their hope on Simon and Helen pay no further attention to them and do what they wish as free agents. For " by his grace men are saved, not by just works " [Eph. 2 : 8]. For actions are just not by nature but by convention, in accordance with the decrees of the angels who made the world and intended to lead men into slavery [cf. Gal. 4 : 9] through precepts of this kind. Therefore he announced that the world would be destroyed and that those who were his would be freed from the rule of those who made the world.‖

Therefore the priests of their mysteries live promiscuously and perform magic, ¶ in so far as each is able to do so. They employ exorcisms and incantations and are constantly occupied with love-philtres, love-magic, familiar spirits, dream-inducers, and other abstruse matters. They have an image of Simon made in the likeness of Zeus and one of Helen in the likeness of Athena, and they worship these. They also bear a name derived from Simon, the founder of their impious doctrine, and are called Simonians, since from them the knowledge of the false name took its beginnings, as one can learn from their own statements.

In addition to this account of the Simonians by Irenaeus, we possess a rather different, and perhaps more original, description provided in the ' Clementine Homilies ' (ii. 22-25).

(22) This Simon's father was Antonius, his mother Rachel. By race he is a Samaritan, from the village of Gitthae, six

---

‡ See p. 28.   § See p. 28.   ‖ See p. 28.
¶ See p. 29.

schoeni [about 30 miles] from the city [of Samaria]. He was very active in Alexandria, Egypt . . . and after gaining great skill in magic and becoming elated, he wished to be regarded as a certain Highest Power, above even the God who made the universe. Sometimes he intimates that he is Christ by calling himself the Standing One. He used this title to indicate that he would always "stand," since there was no cause of corruption which would make his body fail. He says that the God who made the universe is not the highest, and he does not believe that the dead will be raised. He rejects Jerusalem and substitutes Mount Gerezim. Instead of our real Christ he proclaims himself. He allegorises the content of the law in accordance with his own presuppositions and, though he says there will be a judgment, he does not expect one. For if he were convinced that he would be judged by God he would not venture to be impious towards God himself. For this reason some persons—who do not know that, using religion as a cloak, he steals away the essence of the truth, and who faithfully believe the hope and the judgment which he says will somehow take place—go to destruction.

(23) His infiltration of [Christian] religious teaching took place in this way. There was a certain John who baptized every day. In accordance with the doctrine of Pairs he was the forerunner of our Lord Jesus. And as the Lord had twelve apostles, corresponding to the twelve solar months, so also John had thirty leaders totalling up to the monthly reckoning of the moon. In this number was a woman named Helen, so that not even this might lack a special significance. Since a woman is half a man, she made the number of the Thirty incomplete, just as in the case of the moon, whose cycle does not take a complete month. And though Simon was the first and most highly approved of the Thirty in John's view, he did not succeed John after his death for this reason:

(24) Simon was absent in Egypt for the practice of magic when John was killed, and a certain Dositheus, desiring John's Office, falsely announced that Simon was dead and succeeded

to rule over the sect. Not long after, Simon returned and strongly laid claim to the place as his own, though when he met Dositheus he did not demand it back, since he knew that whoever attains power irregularly is not removed. Therefore with assumed friendship he gives himself for a while to the second place under Dositheus. After a few days, however, he took his place among the thirty fellow-disciples and began to slander Dositheus as not having delivered the doctrines correctly. He said that Dositheus did so not because of jealous refusal but because of ignorance. One time Dositheus, who perceived that this artful accusation of Simon was destroying his reputation in the eyes of the majority, so that they did not think he was the Standing One, came in a rage to the usual assembly and, finding Simon, struck him with a staff. The staff seemed to pass through Simon's body as if he were smoke. In amazement Dositheus thereupon says to him, " If you are the Standing One, I too will worship you." When Simon said, " I am," Dositheus, who knew that he himself was not the Standing One, fell down and worshipped; and, associating himself with the twenty-nine leaders, he set Simon in his own place of reputation. Thus, not long afterwards, Dositheus himself, while Simon stood, fell down and died.

(25) Simon goes about in company with Helen and, even until now, as you see, stirs up the crowds. He says that he has brought down this Helen from the highest heavens to the world; she is Queen [*kyria*], since she is all-maternal Being and Wisdom [*Sophia*]. For her sake, he says, the Greeks and the barbarians fought, imagining an image of the truth; for she who really existed was then with the very First God. But by allegorising certain matters of this sort, fictitiously combined with Greek myths, he deceives many, especially by his performance of many marvellous wonders, so that—if we did not know that he does these things by magic—we ourselves would also have been deceived. . . .

---

* *Simon's Syrian contendings with apostles are not mentioned in Acts:*

*they occur, however, in the ' Clementine Homilies ' and ' Recognitions '
and may be derived from Ebionite ' Acts of Peter ': cf. H. J. Schoeps,
' Theologie und Geschichte des Judenchristentums ' (Tübingen, 1949),
37-61. The statue at Rome under Claudius is mentioned by Justin,
Apol. i. 26. 2. Presumably it was really a statue of the god Semo
Sancus. On Simonianism see: L. H. Vincent, " Le culte d'Hélène à
Samarie," ' Revue biblique ' 45 (1936), 221-28; L. Cerfaux, " Simon
le magicien à Samarie," ' Recherches de science religieuse ' 27 (1937),
615-17 ; G. Quispel, " Simon en Helene," ' Nederlands Theologish
Tijdschrift ' 5 (1950-1), 339-45.*

† *Hippolytus (Ref. vi. 19. 6) says Simon taught that he had manifested
himself in these three ways: presumably he is speaking of the fulfilment
of prophecy, Irenaeus of the prophecy to be fulfilled. " Absolute
Sovereignty " occurs in several other systems, as well as in the
' Hermetica ' (see p. 211). Irenaeus now begins over again, perhaps
using another source.*

‡ *The story about Stesichorus, possibly created among Pythagoreans of
the fifth century B.C., is mentioned by Plato, ' Phaedrus ' 243A. In
the story of Simon and Helen it looks like a bit of learning introduced
to give cultural tone to the system. The narrative of salvation is now
continued.*

§ *The picture of Simon's descent closely resembles what is said of the
Saviour-Christ in other gnostic systems and of Jesus Christ in such
relatively " orthodox " documents as the ' Ascension of Isaiah ' and
the ' Epistle of the Apostles.' It seems to combine the Christian idea
of the coming and ascension of Jesus with the gnostic picture of
hostile planetary angels through which the Saviour must somehow
pass.*

‖ *Hostility towards the Old Testament law, occasionally expressed by
the apostle Paul, is reflected in many of the early Christian gnostic
systems, for example those of the Basilidians (Ch. 4), the Carpocratians
(Ch. 5), Cerdo (Ch. 9), and Marcion (Ch. 10). It is analysed not as
reflecting natural law (as Philo of Alexandria had interpreted it) but*

as based on mere convention—a distinction common in Graeco-Roman thought.

¶ *The kinds of magic performed by the Simonians are well known to us from the magical papyri. As for Zeus and Athena, the story of her birth from his head was commonly allegorised in the Graeco-Roman world and she was interpreted as the Wisdom or Forethought which came from the mind of the Father.*

2

Menander (23. 5)

His [Simon's] successor was Menander, a Samaritan who himself reached the pinnacle of the art of magic. He says that the First Power is unknown to all; he himself is the one who was sent down by the invisible [Aeons] as Saviour for the salvation of men. The world was made by angels; like Simon, he says that they were emitted by Thought. He added the gift of magical knowledge given in his teaching so that it might overcome the angels who made the world. His disciples are able to receive resurrection through their baptism into him; they can no longer die but remain ageless and immortal.

It is not altogether clear in what sense Menander can be regarded as a " successor " of Simon Magus, since in this report of his system there is no mention of either Simon or Helen, and Menander himself is the Saviour. His interpretation of baptism looks like a distortion of the Pauline teaching about dying and rising with Christ. With it we may compare the statement of his contemporary, Ignatius bishop of Antioch, that the Eucharist is the "drug of immortality," the " antidote for dying" ('Ephesians' xx. 2). It is possible, of course, that metaphorical language used by both Menander and Ignatius has been misunderstood by their interpreters. In any event, the school of Menander did not " remain ageless and immortal."

3

Saturninus (24. 1-2)

From these teachers both Saturninus, who was from that Antioch which is near Daphne, and Basilides derived their points of departure; but they set forth different doctrines, the one in Syria and the other in Alexandria.

Like Menander, Saturninus sets forth one Father, unknown to all, who made angels, archangels, powers and authorities. The world and everything in it was made by a group of seven angels. Man is the creation of these angels. When a shining image appeared from above, from the Absolute Sovereignty, they were not able to hold it because it immediately returned upward again. They exhorted themselves and said, " Let us make a man after the image and after the likeness " [Gen. 1: 26, deleting " our "]. When he had been made, and what was formed [Gen. 2: 7] could not stand erect because of the angels' weakness but wriggled like a worm, the Power above took pity on him because he was made in its likeness, and it sent a spark of life which raised the man and made him upright and made him live. After death this spark of life returns to what is of the same nature as itself, and the other elements of man's composition are dissolved into what they were made from.

The Saviour is unbegotten, incorporeal, and without form [cf. Is. 53: 2]. He appeared as a man in semblance. The God of the Jews is one of the angels; and because all the Archons willed to destroy their Father, Christ came to destroy the God of the Jews and to save those who believed him. These are the ones who have the spark of life in them. Two kinds of men were formed by the angels—the one evil, the other good. Since the demons were aiding those who were most evil, the Saviour came for the destruction of wicked men and demons and for the salvation of the good.

Marriage and generation are from Satan. (Many of Saturninus' disciples also abstain from animal flesh and lead many astray because of their pretended continence.) Some prophecies were spoken by those angels who made the world, others by Satan. He is an angel, the adversary of those who made the world and especially of the God of the Jews.

With the teaching of Saturninus should be compared that found in the Apocryphon of John (II 2), though my notion that Saturninus could have written the latter document is undoubtedly untenable (cf. H.-C. Puech in W. Schneemelcher—E. Hennecke, ' Neutestamentliche Apokryphen ' I, Tübingen, 1959, 243). All that can be suggested is that Saturninus knew something like this work.

Unlike Simon and Menander, Saturninus advocated a militantly ascetic form of Gnosticism, in which this-worldly magic is entirely rejected and the only goal of the divine " spark of life " is to escape from the world.

4

Basilides (24. 3-6)

But Basilides, in order to seem to have discovered something more exalted and more convincing, extended the teaching of his doctrine into the immeasurable, setting forth Mind, first born from the ungenerated Father; from it was generated Logos; then from Logos, Understanding, from Understanding, Sophia and Power [cf. 1 Cor. 1: 24]; from Power and Sophia the powers and principalities and angels (which he calls " first ") by whom the first heaven was made. Then, deriving their origin from these, others were made; and these made another heaven like the first; and similarly, when still others were made, derived from these, antitypes of those above them, they formed a third heaven. From the third of them, starting down from above, a fourth came into existence, and subsequently in this way still further principalities and angels were made, they say, and a total of 365 heavens. For this reason the year has this many days, in accordance with the number of the heavens.

The angels who control the last heaven, which is visible to us, fashioned everything in the world and made the various parts of the earth and of the nations on it. Their chief is the one who is thought to be the God of the Jews. Since he wanted to subjugate the other nations to his people [the Jews], all the rest of the principalities stood up and resisted him [Ps. 2: 2]; therefore the rest of the nations resisted his nation. The unbegotten and unnamed Father, seeing their destruction, sent his first-born Mind [Christ] to free those who believe him from the power of those who fashioned the world. And to their nations he appeared on earth as a man and worked miracles. Therefore [because he was Mind] he did not suffer, but a certain Simon of Cyrene was impressed to carry his cross for him, and because of ignorance and error he was crucified [cf. Mark 15: 21-24], transfigured by him so that he might be thought to be Jesus: and Jesus himself assumed the form of Simon and, standing by, laughed at them [cf. Ps. 2: 4]. Since he was incorporeal Power and the Mind of the unbegotten Father, he was transfigured in whatever way he wished and thus ascended to him who had sent him, deriding them because he could not be held [cf. Ps. 2: 3] and was invisible to all.

Therefore those who know these things are freed from the world-making principalities. They should not confess the one who was crucified, but him who came in the form of man [cf. Phil. 2: 7] and was thought to be crucified and was called Jesus and was sent by the Father, so that by means of this divine plan he might destroy the works of the world-makers. If anyone confesses the Crucified, he is still a slave and is under the power of those who made bodies. He who denies has been freed from them and knows the plan of the unbegotten Father. There is salvation for the soul alone, since the body is by nature perishable.

The prophecies were spoken by the world-making principalities, and the law by their chief, the one who led the people out of the land of Egypt. They despise meats sacrificed to idols and regard them as nothing [cf. 1 Cor. 10: 19] and use them without any hesitation; they have an " indifferent " use of other actions and of universal lust. They use magic and images and incantations and invocations and all the other things which accompany these.

After inventing certain names as if they belonged to angels, they proclaim that some are in the first heaven, others in the second; then they try to set forth the names, principalities, angels, and powers of the 365 fictitious heavens. The name in which they say the Saviour descended and ascended is Caulacau [Is. 28: 10].* Therefore he who has learned these things and knows all the angels and their sources becomes invisible and incomprehensible to the angels and powers, just as Caulacau was. And as the Son is unknown to all [Matt. 11: 27], so they should be known to no one; but since they all know [cf. 1 Cor. 8: 1] and pass through all, they are invisible and unknown to all. For " you must know everyone, but no one should know you." Therefore men of such a kind are ready to deny and cannot " suffer for the name " [cf. 1 Pet. 4: 14], since they resemble everyone else. " Not many can know these things—one out of a thousand and two out of myriads." And they say that they are no longer Jews but are not yet Christians; it is not right to speak their mysteries at all; one must keep them hidden in silence.

They distribute the positions of the 365 heavens as the astrologers do. Accepting their theorems, they have trans-ferred them into their own form of teaching; their first principle is Abraxas, and therefore has the sum of 365 in itself.

On this description of Basilidian doctrine see R. M. Grant, "Gnostic Origins and the Basilidians of Irenaeus," ' Vigiliae Christianae ' 13 (1959), 121-25. For " no longer Jews " and " invisible to all " see the Nag-Hammadi ' Gospel of Philip ' (H.-M. Schenke in ' Theo-logische Literaturzeitung, 84, 1959, 1-26; sayings 6, 46 and 127), for " one out of a thousand and two out of ten thousand " see the ' Gospel of Thomas,' saying 24 Leipoldt. The Greek equivalent of A is 1, of B 2, of X 60, of R 100, and of S 200; total, 365. A quite different picture of Basilidian doctrine is provided by Hippolytus; see Part IV.

* The Hebrew word is sometimes translated "precept upon precept"; for another Gnostic interpretation see p. 107.

5

Carpocrates (25)

A. CARPOCRATES

Carpocrates says that the universe and its contents were made
by angels much inferior to the unbegotten Father, but that
Jesus was begotten by Joseph and, having come into existence
like other men, became more righteous than the rest. When
his soul became vigorous and pure it remembered what it had
seen in its circuit [Plato, *Phaedrus* 248A] with the unbegotten
God, and therefore power was sent it by him so that it could
escape the world-creators by means of it and so that by passing through all, free among them all, it might come to him,
similarly accepting what was like it. They say that the soul
of Jesus was brought up lawfully in Jewish customs but
despised them and therefore received powers through which
it annihilated the passions which are attached to men and
punish them. (2) The soul which, like the soul of Christ, is able
to despise the world-creating archons will similarly receive
power to do similar things. For this reason they have reached
such a state of pride that they say they are like Jesus himself;
but some say that they are even more powerful, and others say
that they surpass his disciples, such as Peter and Paul and the
rest of the apostles; they fall short of Jesus in no respect. Their
souls, having come from the Authority above, and therefore
similarly despising the world-creators, were deemed worthy of
the same power and worthy to attain the same end. If anyone
despises things below more than Jesus did, he can become
greater than he was.

(3) They practise magic arts and incantations, charms and spells, familiar spirits and dream-senders, and all other wicked activities, saying that they have power to rule over the rulers and makers of this world and also over all that they created. Like the Gentiles, they were driven by Satan to slander the divine name of the Church so that men who hear of their actions of one sort or another suppose that we are all of the same kind and turn their ears away from the proclamation of the truth. Seeing what they do, men blaspheme all of us, though we participate with them in nothing—doctrine, practice, daily life. But they lead a luxurious life and have an irreligious outlook; they misuse our name as a cloak for their wickedness [cf. 1 Pet. 2: 16]; " their condemnation is just " [Rom. 3: 8], and they receive from God a retribution worthy of their works.

They have reached such a pitch of madness that they say that it is in their power to do whatever is irreligious and impious, for they say that actions are good and bad only in accordance with human opinion. In the transmigrations into bodies, souls ought to experience every kind of life and action, if in a single life on earth any one of them has not first taken care to experience everything once for all and in equal completeness [actions such as it is not right for us to mention or to hear or even to have in mind, or to believe that any such thing is considered among men who live in the civilised world], so that, according to what their writings say, their souls, which have been involved in every experience, may not, when they depart, still suffer any lack. They must act in such a way that they will not be forced into another body if something is still lacking in their freedom.

For this reason, they say, Jesus told this parable: " When you are with your adversary on the way, act so that you may be freed from him, lest he deliver you to the judge and the judge to the officer and he cast you into prison; verily I say to you, you will not come out from there until you pay the last quadrant " [Luke 12: 58-59; Matt. 5: 25-26]. They say that the " adversary " is one of the angels who are in the

world; they call him the Devil and they say that he was made
in order to lead souls which have perished from the world to
the " prince." They say that he is the first of the world-
makers, and that he " delivers " such souls to another angel,
who is his " officer," in order to enclose them in other bodies.
They call the body a "prison" [cf. Plato, *Cratylus* 400C]. And
the saying, " You will not come out from there until you pay
the last quadrant," they explain as meaning that no one
leaves the power of those angels who made the world; souls
are always made reincarnate until they have completed all
sins; when nothing is lacking, then the freed soul departs to
[cf. Luke 12: 58] the God above the world-creating angels, and
thus all souls will be saved. The souls which in a single life on
earth manage to participate in all sins will no longer become
reincarnate but, having paid all their " debts," will be freed
so that they no longer come to be in a body.

(5) And if godless, unlawful, and unspeakable things are
done by them, I should not believe [them?]. But in their
writings it is written, and they provide exegesis to prove, that
Jesus spoke in a mystery privately to his disciples and apostles
[Mark 4: 10-11] and judged them worthy to transmit these
things to those who were worthy and who believed them. For
through faith and love [cf. Gal. 5: 6] we are saved; all else is
indifferent, after the opinion of men, and is sometimes considered good, sometimes bad. Nothing is evil by nature.

(6) Some of them cauterise their disciples behind the lobe
of the right ear. When Marcellina came to Rome under
Anicetus, since she belonged to this school she led many astray.
They call themselves Gnostics. They have images, some
painted, some made of other materials, and they say that their
picture of Christ was made by Pilate when Jesus was among
men. They put crowns on these and place them with images
of worldly philosophers like Pythagoras and Plato and Aristotle
and the others; and the rest of their veneration of the images
is like that of the Gentiles.

In addition to this account of the Carpocratians by Irenaeus, we possess a slightly more philosophical defence of promiscuity as based on the law of God, which is identified with the law of nature, not with the decalogue. It was written by Carpocrates' son Epiphanes.

B. EPIPHANES, CONCERNING RIGHTEOUSNESS (JUSTICE)

The " righteousness " [justice] of God is a kind of sharing along with equality. There is equality in the heaven which is stretched out in all directions and contains the entire earth in its circle. The night reveals all the stars equally. The light of the sun, which is the cause of the daytime and the father of light, God pours out from above [cf. James 1 : 17] upon the earth in equal measure to all who have power to see. For all see alike, since here is no distinction between rich and poor, people and governor, stupid and clever, female and male, free men and slaves. Even the irrational animals are not accorded any different treatment; but in just the same way God pours out from above sunlight equally upon all the animals. He establishes his justice to both good and bad by seeing that none is able to get more than his share and to deprive his neighbour, so that he has twice the light his neighbour has. The sun causes food to grow for all living beings alike; the universal justice is given to all equally. In this respect there is no difference between the species of oxen and particular oxen, between the species of pigs and particular pigs, between the species of sheep and particular sheep, and so on with all the rest. In them universality is manifest as justice. Furthermore all plants " after their kind " are sown equally in the earth. Common nourishment grows for all beasts which feed on the earth's produce; to all it is alike. It is regulated by no law, but rather is harmoniously available to all through the gift of him who gave it and commanded it to grow [Gen. 1 : 11-12, 22].

And for birth there is no written law; otherwise it would have been transcribed. All beings beget and give birth alike, having received by justice an innate equality. The Creator and Father of all with his own justice appointed this, just as he gave equally the eye to all to enable them to see. He did not make a distinction between female and male, rational and irrational, nor between anything and anything else at all; rather he shared out sight equally and universally. It was given to all alike by a single command.

As the laws could not punish men who were ignorant of them, they taught men to transgress [cf. Gal. 4: 19]. For particularity of the laws cut up and destroyed the universal equality of the divine law. . . .

The ideas of Mine and Thine crept in [cf. Gal. 2: 4] through the laws which cause the earth, money, and even marriage no longer to bring forth fruit for common use. For God made vines for all to use in common, since they do not refuse the sparrow or the thief; and similarly wheat and the other fruits. But outlawed sharing and the vestiges of equality generated the thief of domestic animals and fruits.

For man God made all things to be common property. He brought the female to be with the male in common and in the same way united all the animals. He thus showed " righteousness " to be a universal sharing along with equality. But those who have been born in this way have denied the sharing which is the corollary of their origin and say, " Let him who has taken one woman keep her," whereas all can share her, just as the other animals show us.

With a view to the permanence of the race, he has implanted in males a strong and ardent desire which neither law nor custom nor any other restraint is able to destroy. For it is God's decree. . . . Consequently one must understand the saying " Thou shalt not desire " as if the lawgiver was making a jest, to which he added the even more comic words " thy neighbour's goods " [Exod. 20: 17]. For he himself who gave the desire to sustain the race orders that it is to be suppressed, though he removes it from no other animals. And by the words " thy neighbour's wife " he says something even more ludicrous, since he forces what should be common property to be treated as a private possession [Clement, *Strom.* iii. 6–9].

6

Cerinthus (26. 1)

A certain Cerinthus in Asia taught that the world was made
not by the first God but by a certain power clearly separate
and distinct from the Power above all, and ignorant of the
God above all. He supposed that Jesus was born not of a
virgin but of Joseph and Mary [Luke 2: 33, etc.], like all other
men, and he became more righteous, more prudent, and more
wise [Luke 2: 40, 52] than all. After his baptism, from the
Absolute Sovereignty above all the Christ descended upon
him in the form of a dove [Luke 3: 22]; then he proclaimed
the unknown Father [cf. Luke 10: 22] and worked miracles.
At the end, the Christ withdrew from Jesus [Luke 23: 46];
Jesus suffered [Luke 23: 47] and was raised, but the Christ
remained impassible, since he was spiritual.

*Two other passages about Cerinthian doctrine deserve quotation; both
reflect concern about apocalyptic eschatology. (1) " After the resurrection the kingdom of Christ will be on earth, and the flesh, dwelling
at Jerusalem, will once more serve lusts and pleasures (cf. Tit. 3: 3).
There will be a period of a thousand years to be spent in wedding
festivities " (Gaius in Eusebius, ' Hist. Eccl.,' iii. 28. 2; a hostile
account, relating Cerinthus to the book of Revelation). (2) " Christ
suffered and was crucified but has not yet been raised; he will rise at
the general resurrection of the dead " (Epiphanius, ' Pan.' xxviii. 6. 1;
caution is needed in using this account, since its author confuses Cerinthus
with the Ebionites).*

7

The Ebionites (26. 2)

Those who are called Ebionites acknowledge that the world was made by God, but their attitude towards the Lord is like that of Cerinthus and Carpocrates. They use only the gospel which is according to Matthew, and they reject the apostle Paul, calling him an apostate from the law. They endeavour to interpret the prophetic writings in a rather speculative way. They are circumcised and they persevere in the practices of the law and in a Jewish manner of life to such an extent that they venerate Jerusalem as the house of God.

It appears that in the time, or in the sources, of Irenaeus, Ebionite teachings had not yet been developed in the " gnosticizing " direction reflected in the Pseudo-Clementine ' Homilies ' (and ' Recognitions ') of the fourth century, as well as in the description provided by Epiphanius (' Panarion,' 30). This direction may be implied, however, in Irenaeus' mention of their " speculative " exegesis. On the later Ebionites see H. J. Schoeps, ' Theologie und Geschichte des Judenchristentums ' (Tübingen, 1949); 'Aus frühchristlicher Zeit' (Tubingen, 1950); M. Simon, ' Verus Israel ' (Paris, 1948), 276-314; J. Daniélou, ' Théologie du Judéo-Christianisme ' (Paris, 1958).

8

The Nicolaitans (26. 3)

The Nicolaitans have as their master Nicolaus, one of the seven who were first ordained to the diaconate by the apostles [Acts 6: 5]; they live promiscuously. Who they are is most fully revealed in the Revelation of John [2: 6, 15]; they teach that fornication is a matter of indifference and that one should eat meats sacrificed to idols. Therefore the Word has spoken of them thus: " But you have this, that you hate the works of the Nicolaitans, which I also hate."

Actually it is by no means clear that the Nicolaus of Acts had anything to do with the Nicolaitans of Revelation. Hippolytus (' Ref.' vii. 36. 3) and Epiphanius (' Pan.' xxv. 1) accept Irenaeus' conjecture; Clement (' Strom.' iii. 26. 1), Eusebius (' Hist. Eccl.' iii. 29. 1), and Pseudo-Ignatius (' Trall.' xi. 2) reject it. The stories about Nicolaus told by the later anti-heretical writers look like legends, and Epiphanius' account of Nicolaitan doctrine and practice seems to be based partly on his own fertile imagination, partly on what he knows about other groups.

9

Cerdo (27. 1)

And a certain Cerdo, originating from the Simonians, came to Rome under Hyginus [who held the office of bishop ninth in succession from the apostles] and taught that the one who was proclaimed as God by the law and the prophets is not the Father of our Lord Jesus Christ. The [Old Testament] God is known; the Father is unknown. The former is just, while the latter is good.

In Irenaeus' opinion, as is clear not only from this section but also from the following one (Ch. 10), Marcionite dualism was based on the dualistic (Simonian) teaching of his predecessor Cerdo. Scholars like Harnack who have minimised Gnostic elements in Marcion's thought have come close to denying Cerdo's existence; but there is no real reason for supposing that Irenaeus was misinformed.

10

Marcion (27. 2-3)

(2) Marcion of Pontus succeeded Cerdo and developed his doctrine, shamelessly blaspheming him who was proclaimed as God by the law and the prophets and calling him the creator of evil things [Is. 45: 7], desirous of wars, inconstant in purpose [Gen. 6: 6], and inconsistent with himself. From the Father, who is above the God who made the world, Jesus came to Judaea in the time of the governor Pontius Pilate, procurator for Tiberius Caesar, and was manifested in the form of a man to those who were in Judaea; he destroyed the prophets and the law [cf. Matt. 5: 17] and all the works of that God who made the world, whom Marcion calls Cosmo-crator [world-ruler]. Furthermore, Marcion circumcises the gospel according to Luke and takes out everything written about the generation of the Lord [Luke 1: 1—2: 52], as well as many items about the teaching of the Lord's words in which the Lord is most plainly described as acknowledging the Creator of this universe as his Father. He persuaded his disciples that he himself was more trustworthy than the apostles who transmitted the gospel; but he delivered to them not the gospel but a particle of the gospel. Similarly he abridged the epistles of the apostle Paul, taking out whatever was clearly said by the apostle concerning that God who made the world [since this God is the Father of our Lord Jesus Christ] as well as whatever the apostle taught when he mentioned passages from the prophetic writings which foretell the Lord's coming.

(3) He says that there will be salvation only for souls which have learned his doctrine; the body, doubtless because it was taken from the earth [Gen. 2: 7], cannot participate in salvation. To this blasphemy against God he adds the following story, truly assuming the role of the devil and saying everything contrary to the truth. When the Lord descended to Hades, Cain and those like him, the Sodomites, the Egyptians, and those like them, and in general all the peoples who have walked in every compound of wickedness, were saved by him; they ran to him and were taken up into his kingdom. But Abel, Enoch, Noah, and the rest of the righteous, and the patriarchs related to Abraham, along with all the prophets and those who pleased God, did not participate in salvation. [The serpent who was in Marcion proclaimed this!] For since they knew [he says] that their God was always testing them, and suspected that he was testing them then, they did not run to Jesus nor did they believe his proclamation; and therefore [he said] their souls remained in Hades. . . .

On Marcion cf. A. v. Harnack, ' Marcion: das Evangelium vom fremden Gott ' (ed. 2, Leipzig, 1924); this remains indispensable because of its very full collection of Marcionite fragments. See also J. Knox, ' Marcion and the New Testament ' (Chicago, 1942); E. C. Blackman, ' Marcion and his Influence ' (London, 1948).

The Encratites and Tatian (28)

From the aforementioned persons, many offshoots of many heresies have come into existence because many—or indeed all —of them wish to be teachers and to leave the sect in which they were; composing another doctrine from another opinion, and then another from another, they drive onwards to teach in a new way, describing themselves as the discoverers of whatever opinion they have concocted.

From Saturninus and Marcion the so-called Encratites [continent ones] have proclaimed celibacy, rejecting the ancient work of God in forming mankind and implicitly blaming him for making male and female for the generation of men. And they introduced abstinence from eating what they call " animate " food, ungrateful to the God who made all. They deny the salvation of the first-formed man—this is now their new discovery! A certain Tatian first introduced this blasphemy; he had been a hearer of Justin, and as long as he was with him he expressed nothing of this sort; but after Justin's martyrdom [c. 165] he left the church. He was inflated by the idea of being a teacher and by the notion that he was superior to others, so he established his own form of doctrine. He invented certain invisible Aeons like those of Valentinus, attacked marriage as corruption and fornication [like Marcion and Saturninus], and denied the salvation of Adam.

Others, on the other hand, starting from Basilides and Carpocrates, introduced promiscuous intercourse and many marriages and indifference about eating meats sacrificed to idols; they said that God does not really care about these matters.

Indeed, there is no space to speak about those who in one way or another have departed from the truth.

On Tatian and Encratism see F. Bolgiani in ' Atti della Accademia delle Scienze di Torino,' 91 (1956-57), 1-77.

12

The Barbelo-Gnostics (29)

At this point in his discussion Irenaeus turns aside to provide further examples of Gnostic doctrines from systems known to him from Gnostic writings. His account of the Barbelo-Gnostic doctrine is derived from a Greek text of the 'Secret Book of John' (see Part II. 2), as Carl Schmidt first pointed out ('Philotesia Paul Kleinert,' Berlin, 1907, 315-36). Either Irenaeus' source did not contain the elaborate Christian framework it now has or, more probably, Irenaeus himself preferred not to make mention of it.

There is a never-ageing Aeon in a Virginal Spirit which is called Barbelo; the unnameable Father is also there. He wished to reveal himself to Barbelo. This Thought came forth and stood in his sight and asked for Foreknowledge. When Foreknowledge had also come forth, then they both requested Imperishability, and she came forth; then Eternal Life. Barbelo rejoiced in them and, looking towards the Greatness and delighting in the Conception, she bore a Light like it. This was the Beginning of the illumination and generation of all things.

When the Father saw this Light he anointed it with his own goodness so that it would be perfect. This is Christ [" anointed "]. He then asked that a helper, Mind, be given him, and Mind came forth. Then the Father emitted Logos. Next there were unions of Thought and Logos, Imperishability and Christ; Eternal Life was joined with Will and Mind with Foreknowledge. These emanations magnified the great Light and Barbelo. Afterwards, from Thought and Logos was emitted Self-Born as a representation of the great Light; it was greatly honoured and all things were subjected to it. With it was emitted Truth, and thus there was another pair, Self-Born and Truth. From the Light which is Christ and from Imperishability four luminaries were emitted to stand about Self-Born; again, from Will and Eternal Life four emissions took place to serve the four luminaries which are called Grace, Willing, Intelligence, and Thinking. Grace was united with the great first Light, which is Saviour and is called Armogen; Willing with the second, called Raguel; Intelligence with the third, called David; Thinking with the fourth, called Eleleth. When all of these had been established, Self-Born also emitted the Perfect and True Man, who is also called Adamas because he is adamant, as his sources are, though he was separated from the first Light by Armogen. Perfect Knowledge [gnosis] was emitted by Self-Born along with the Man, and was joined to him; from her he knows the one who is above all. Unconquered Power was given him by the Virginal Spirit in which all things rest to praise the great Aeon.

Thus were revealed the Mother, the Father, and the Son: from the Man and Knowledge was born the Tree, which is also called Knowledge [gnosis].

Then from the first angel which is with Monogenes [Self-Born] was emitted Holy Spirit, which is also called Sophia and Prunicos. When this spirit saw that all the rest had partners but she did not, she sought someone with whom to be united. When she found none, she was extended and looked down to the lower regions in the belief that she would find one there. When she found none, she leaped back, wearied because she had made this effort without the good will of the Father. Afterwards, driven by simplicity and kindness, she generated a work in which were Ignorance and Presumption. This work is called Proarchon, the fashioner of this universe. He stole a great power from his mother and departed from her to the lower regions and made the firmament of heaven, in which he dwells. And since he is Ignorance, he made the powers beneath him: angels, firmaments, and everything earthly. Then he was united with Presumption and generated Wickedness, Jealousy, Envy, Strife,* and Desire. When they were generated, the Mother Sophia fled in grief and withdrew above; she became the Eight for those who count from below. When she withdrew, he thought he was alone, and therefore he said, " I am a jealous God, and there is none but me " [Exod. 20: 5, etc.].

* Cf. G. Zuntz in 'Journal of Theological Studies' N.S. 6 (1955), 232-44.

13

The Sethian-Ophites (30)

Another Gnostic reinterpretation of the Old Testament story is provided by Irenaeus in his account of the doctrines of the Sethian-Ophites. Seth was the only child of Adam and Eve from whom gnostics could trace their descent; the serpent [ophis], according to some of them, was really Sophia, opposed to Ialdabaoth. This account differs in detail from the ' Secret Book of John ' but its basic point is the same.

For a bibliography on the Ophites, see Part III. 1; on this myth and parallels, see H.-C. Puech, " Archontiker ", ' Reallexikon für Antike und Christentum,' I, 633-43; G. Quispel, " Die oudste vorm van de gnostische mythe," ' Nederlands Theologische Tijdschrift ' 8 (1953-54), 20-25.

There is a certain First Light in the Depth; this is the Father of All, who is called the First Man. The coming forth of his Thought is the emission of the Son of Man, the Second Man. Below these two is the Holy Spirit, and beneath her are the various elements—water, darkness, abyss, chaos [Gen. 1 : 2]—over which the Spirit was borne, the First Woman. Then the First Man with his Son rejoiced over the beauty of the female Spirit, and he illuminated her and from her generated an imperishable Light, the Third Man, who is called Christ, the Son of the First and Second Man and the Holy Spirit, the First Woman, when the Father and Son lay with the Woman, who is called the Mother of the Living [Gen. 3 : 20]. But when she was unable to carry or receive the greatness of the

Light, it overflowed to the regions of the Left side. Thus their only Son, Christ, is the Right side and the Ascension and was immediately drawn up to the Imperishable Aeon, which is the true and holy Church, the Calling and Assembly and Union of the Father of All, the First Man, with the Son, the Second Man, and with Christ, the Son of these two and the Woman.

The Power which overflowed from the Woman and has the moist nature of light, fell from above, from its fathers. By its own will it has the moist nature of light, and is called Left and Prunicos and Sophia and Male-Female. It came down directly upon the waters, when they were motionless, and set them in motion, moving boldly as far as the abysses; and it took a body for itself from them. Everything ran together and adhered to the moist nature of the Power's light, and enclosed it; if everything had not possessed it, all things might have been completely absorbed and submerged by matter. When it was bound and weighed down by the body of matter, it lay low, though it tried to escape from the waters and ascend to the Mother, though it could not do so because of the weight of the surrounding body. Since it was in such an unfortunate condition it tried to hide the light which had come from above, fearing that the light would be injured by the lower elements as it itself had been. And when it received power from the moist nature of the light which was with it, it leaped back and was borne upwards to the Height. When it had ascended, it spread out and became a covering and formed the visible heaven out of its body; and it remained under the heaven which it made, retaining the form of a watery body. But when it acquired a desire for the Light above, and was constantly gaining power, it put off its body and was freed from it. This body is called female, after the First Woman.

Her Son had in himself a certain aspiration towards the Imperishable [Aeon]; this had been left in him by the Mother, who works through it. Becoming potent, he himself emitted from the waters a son without a mother; for he did not know the Mother. The second son emitted a son who was an imitation of his father; this third one generated a fourth, and the fourth himself generated a son; from the fifth a sixth son was generated, and the sixth generated a seventh. Thus the Seven was completed among them [cf. Gen. 2: 1-2]; the Mother has the eighth place. Their dignities and powers correspond to their order of generation.

The one who is first from the Mother is Ialdabaoth; the next, Iao; the next, Sabaoth; the fourth, Adonaios [Adonai]; the fifth, Eloeus [Elohim]; the sixth, Oreus; the seventh and most recent of all, Astaphaeus. These heavens and excellences and powers and angels have places in heaven according to the order of their generation, and they invisibly reign over things celestial and terrestrial. The first of them, Ialdabaoth, despised the Mother in that without her permission he made sons and grandsons—angels, archangels, excellences, powers, and dominions. When they had been made, his sons turned to a struggle against him for the primacy. Therefore in grief and despair Ialdabaoth looked down on the dregs of matter and solidified his desire into it and generated a son. This son is Mind, twisted in the form of a serpent [*ophis*, hence Ophites], and is also Spirit and Soul and everything worldly. From him were generated all forgetfulness and wickedness and jealousy and envy and death. The Father [Ialdabaoth] drove out this serpent-shaped and twisted Mind [cf. Gen. 3: 14] because of its crookedness, all the more because it had once been with his Father in heaven and in paradise. For this reason Ialdabaoth exulted, boasting because all these were beneath him, and said, " I am Father and God, and above me is no one " [cf. Is. 44: 6). The Mother heard and cried out against him, " Do not speak falsely, Ialdabaoth; above you are the Father of All, the First Man, and the Man who is Son of Man." When all things were disturbed because of the new voice and the inconceivable address, and they were asking whence the call had come, Ialdabaoth said, in order to summon them and draw them to himself, " Come, let us make a man in our image " [Gen. 1: 26].

The six powers heard these words, and when the Mother gave them the idea of man so that through him she might drive them out from the principal power, they came together and formed a man who was immeasurable in breadth and length. When he did nothing but writhe, they bore him to his Father [Ialdabaoth], while Sophia managed to deprive him [Ialdabaoth] of the moist nature of Light so that he could not be raised up against those who are above, by possessing power; he [Ialdabaoth] breathed into man the breath of life [Gen. 2:7] and was thus secretly deprived of the power; hence man had Mind and Desire, and these are the parts of man which are saved. Immediately he gave thanks to the First Man, abandoning his makers.

The jealous Ialdabaoth wanted a plan for depriving man [of the moist nature of Light] through woman, and from his own desire he brought forth a woman whom Prunicos [Sophia] took and invisibly deprived of power. The others came and admired her beauty [Gen. 6:2] and called her Eve; they desired her and from her generated sons who are called angels. But their Mother [Sophia] planned to seduce Adam and Eve through a serpent so that they would transgress the command-ment of Ialdabaoth. Eve, hearing this word as if it came [directly] from the Son of God, readily believed it and per-suaded Adam to eat from the tree of which God [Ialdabaoth] had said not to eat. When they ate, they knew the Power which is above all and they departed from those who had made them.

When Prunicos saw that the powers were overcome by her creatures, she rejoiced greatly and again exclaimed that, since the Father was imperishable, Ialdabaoth spoke falsely when he called himself " Father "; and since the Man and the First Woman had already existed, she [Eve] sinned when she com-mitted adultery [with angels]. But Ialdabaoth, because of the forgetfulness which surrounded him, paid no attention to her exclamation but cast Adam and Eve out of paradise, since they had transgressed his commandment. He had wanted to generate sons from Eve, but he did not succeed, since his Mother opposed him in every way and secretly deprived Adam and Eve of the moist nature of light, so that the Spirit

from the Highest Power might not share in the curse or the
disgrace. Thus they were emptied of divine substance, cursed
by Ialdabaoth, and made to fall from heaven into this world.
The serpent, too, who had worked against his Father, was cast
down into the lower world by him. He [the serpent] brought
the angels who are here under his power and generated six
sons; he himself is the seventh, in imitation of the Seven
which is about the Father. These are the seven worldly
demons, forever opposing and resisting the human race; for
their sake their father was cast down below.

   At first Adam and Eve had light and bright bodies,
" spiritual bodies," as they were formed originally. When they
came to this place, they became darker and thicker and more
sluggish. The soul, too, became lax and languid. And since
they had received only a " worldly " breathing from their
maker, Prunicos took pity on them and gave them the odour
of the sweetness of the moist nature of light. Through this they
came to remembrance of themselves; they recognised that
they were naked and knew the material nature of the body
[Gen. 3: 7], and they knew that they bore the burden of
death; but they were patient, recognising that the body contained them only for a time. They found food to eat by the
guidance of Sophia, and when they were filled they had sexual
intercourse and generated Cain. Cain was immediately taken
and overthrown by the serpent which was cast down, and by
the serpent's [six] sons. The serpent filled him with worldly
forgetfulness and brought him to stupidity and presumption
so that when he killed his brother Abel he might be the first
example of jealousy and death. After these, by the providence
of Prunicos, Seth was generated and then Norea.* All the
rest of mankind was generated from them. By the lower
Seven mankind was brought into all wickedness, and to
apostasy from the holy Seven above, and to idolatry and to
every kind of contempt. Since the Mother was always invisibly
opposing the lower Seven, she saved what was her own, i.e.,
the moist nature of light.

   * For attempts to explain her existence cf. Epiphanius, *Pan.* 26, 1., 3-5.

The [lower]† Seven consists of the seven stars called planets, and the serpent who was cast down has two names, Michael and Samael.

Ialdabaoth was angry with men because they did not worship or honour him as Father and God; he sent a deluge upon them to destroy all of them at the same time. But Sophia withstood him at this point, too, and saved those who were with Noah in the ark because of the moist nature of that light which originated from her; through it the world was again filled with men. One of these, named Abraham, was chosen by Ialdabaoth himself, who gave him a covenant to the effect that if his seed persevered in serving him, he would give it the earth as an inheritance. Later through Moses he led the descendants of Abraham out of Egypt and gave them a law and made them Jews; from that time the seven days were chosen which make up the holy Seven [week]. And each one of them [the Seven] chose his own herald to glorify and proclaim him as God, so that the others might hear the praises and serve the gods proclaimed through the prophets.

Thus Moses was the prophet of Ialdabaoth, as were Joshua, Amos and Habakkuk; Samuel, Nathan, Jonah, and Micah were prophets of Iao; Elijah, Joel, and Zechariah were prophets of Sabaoth; Isaiah, Ezekiel, Jeremiah, and Daniel were prophets of Adonai; Tobias and Haggai were prophets of Eloi; Micah and Nahum were prophets of Oreus; and Ezra and Zephaniah were prophets of Astanfeus.

Each one of these glorified his own Father and God, but Sophia spoke many things through them concerning the First Man and the Imperishable Aeon and the Christ who is above, forewarning and preserving men for the imperishable Light and the First Man and the descent of Christ. When the Archons were terrified by these words and marvelled at the novelty in what the prophets proclaimed, Prunicos effected (through Ialdabaoth, who was ignorant of what he did) the emission of two men, one from the sterile Elizabeth, the other from the virgin Mary. And since she [Sophia] found no rest,

† Holy [text].

either in heaven or on earth [cf. Enoch 42], she was sorrowful and called for the help of her Mother. Her Mother, the First Woman, took pity on the repentance of her daughter, and asked the First Man to send Christ to her to help; he was emitted and descended to his sister and to the moist nature of light.

When the Sophia below recognised that her brother descended to her, she proclaimed his coming through John and prepared the baptism of repentance and made Jesus suitable in advance so that the descending Christ might find a pure vessel, and so that through her son Ialdabaoth the Woman might be proclaimed by Christ. He descended through the seven heavens, and was made like their sons, and gradually deprived them of their power. All the moist nature of light ran together to him, and Christ, descending into this world, first put on his sister Sophia [as a robe], and both rejoiced in mutual comfort; they are the Bridegroom and the Bride.

Jesus was generated from the virgin through the working of God [Ialdabaoth?]; he was wiser and purer and more righteous than all [other] men; Christ combined with Sophia descended [into him] and thus Jesus became Christ.

Many of his disciples did not recognise the descent of Christ into him; but when Christ descended into Jesus, then he began to work miracles and to heal and to proclaim the unknown Father and to confess himself openly as the Son of the First Man. Because of this the powers and the Father of Jesus were angry, and they took steps to kill him. When he was led to death, the Christ with Sophia departed to the Imperishable Aeon, while Jesus was crucified. Christ did not forget what was his own, but from above sent into him a certain power which raised him in a body which was both psychic and spiritual; the worldly elements remained in the world. When the disciples saw that he [the transformed Jesus] had risen again, they did not recognise him [Luke 24: 34], nor did they recognise the Christ* by whose grace he rose from the dead. And the greatest error of the disciples was this, that they

---

* Irenaeus has "Jesus."

thought he rose in a worldly [material] body, and did not know that " flesh and blood do not attain to the kingdom of God " [1 Cor. 15: 50]. The descent and ascent of the Christ is confirmed by the fact that the disciples say that Jesus did nothing remarkable either before the baptism or after the resurrection. They are ignorant of the union of Jesus with the Christ and of the Imperishable Aeon with the Seven. [The " worldly body " is that which living beings have.] Jesus remained for eighteen months after the resurrection and from the perception which descended into him learned [this teaching] which is manifest. He taught these things to a few of his disciples who, he knew, could receive [Matt. 19: 11] such great mysteries [Matt. 13: 11], and thus was taken up into heaven.

Christ sits at the right hand of the Father Ialdabaoth in order to receive to himself the souls of those who have known them, after they have put off the worldly flesh. Christ enriches himself (though his Father is ignorant of him and does not even see him), so that the more Jesus enriches himself with holy souls, the less his Father becomes deprived of his power through the souls. For he [Christ] will not receive holy souls to send them back to the world; he will receive only those which are of substance, i.e., from the " breathing." The end will come when the whole moist nature of the spirit of light is collected and withdrawn into the Aeon of Imperishability.

Some of them say that the serpent was Sophia herself; for this reason it was opposed to the maker of Adam and gave knowledge to men, and therefore is called the wisest of all [Gen. 3: 1]. And the position of our intestines through which food is taken in, and their shape, shows that the hidden Mother of the shape of the serpent is a substance within us.

14

The Cainites (31. 1-2)

Others, whom they call Cainites, say that Cain was from the Absolute Sovereignty above, and they acknowledge Esau, Korah, and the Sodomites, along with all persons of this kind, as their own. These were hated by the Creator because they suffered no harm [from him], for Sophia took to herself what was her own in them.

And they say that the betrayer Judas was the only one of the apostles who possessed this knowledge. For this reason he brought about the mystery of the betrayal; through him all things on earth and in heaven were destroyed. They put forward a work to this effect called the *Gospel of Judas*.

I myself have read writings of theirs in which they advocate the destruction of the words of the Womb [for they call the Creator of heaven and earth " Womb "]. They cannot be saved unless they experience everything, as Carpocrates also said. At each of these sinful and disgusting actions an angel is present, not only to hear of the boldness but to cause the uncleanness of the agent. They express the meaning of the action by invoking the angel: " O angel, I consume your work completely; O power, I perform your action." And this is " perfect knowledge," to undertake without fear such actions as should not even be mentioned.

A few additional details may be noted from later writers. (1) " Judas, observing that Christ wished to betray the truth, betrayed him so that

the truth could not be betrayed " (*Pseudo-Tertullian*, ' *Adv. omn. haer.*'
2). (*2*) " *Abel was from the weaker power* " (*Epiphanius*, ' *Pan.*,'
xxxviii. 1, 2). (*3*) " *This is the angel who blinded Moses and these
are the angels who hid and resurrected those about Korah and Dathan
and Abiron* " (*ibid., 2. 4*). (*4*) " *They invent another treatise in the
name of the apostle Paul . . . which they call the Ascension of Paul* "
(*ibid., 2. 5; cf. 2 Cor. 12: 2-3*). *For an attempt to explain the name
" Womb " from Exodus 34: 6 see " Notes on Gnosis," ' Vigiliae
Christianae* ' *10* (*1957*), *146-47.*

PART II

THE GNOSTIC WRITINGS
OF THE COPTIC PAPYRUS
BEROLINENSIS 8502

This Coptic papyrus, probably found near Achmim in Egypt, was bought for the Berlin Museum in 1896. It was written in the fifth century of our era and contains the Gospel of Mary, the ' Secret Book of John,' the Sophia of Jesus Christ, and the Acts of Peter. The first three writings are Gnostic, and they were first published, with a German translation, by Walter Till in ' Die gnostischen Schriften des koptischen Papyrus Berolinensis 8502' (Berlin, 1955). The translation of the following selections, made from Till's German, has been revised in relation to the Coptic text by Professor E. R. Hardy.

A fragment of the Gospel of Mary written in Greek in the third century was published by C. H. Roberts in the ' Catalogue of the Greek and Latin Papyri in the John Rylands Library,' III. (Manchester, 1938), No. 463. The original form of this document and of the Apocryphon of John probably come from the second century. In 1907 Carl Schmidt (' Philotesia Kleinert,' 315-36) pointed out that a chapter in Irenaeus (' Adv. haer.' i., 29; section 13 above) is probably based on the Greek original version of the Apocryphon. In the Gnostic library found at Nag-Hammadi there are three more Coptic versions of it.

The Gospel of Mary

[*The Coptic papyrus, from which the first six pages have been lost, begins in the middle of this gospel.*]

". . . will, then, matter be saved or not?"

The Saviour said, "All natures, all formed things, all creatures exist in and with one another and will again be resolved into their own roots, because the nature of matter is dissolved into the roots of its nature alone. He who has ears to hear, let him hear" [cf. Matt. 11: 15, etc.].

Peter said to him, "Since you have now explained all things to us, tell us this: what is the sin of the world?" [cf. John 1: 29].

The Saviour said, "Sin as such does not exist, but you make sin when you do what is of the nature of fornication, which is called 'sin.' For this reason the Good came into your midst, to the essence of each nature, to restore it to its root." He went on to say, "For this reason you come into existence and die [. . .] whoever knows may know [. . .] a suffering which has nothing like itself, which has arisen out of what is contrary to nature. Then there arises a disturbance in the whole body. For this reason I said to you, Be of good courage [cf. Matt. 28: 9], and if you are discouraged, still take courage over against the various forms of nature. He who has ears to hear, let him hear." When the Blessed One had said this, he greeted all of them, saying "Peace be with you [cf. John 14: 27]. Receive my peace for yourselves. Take heed lest anyone lead you astray with the words, ' Lo, here! ' or ' Lo, there! ' [cf. Matt. 24: 5, 23; Luke 17: 21] for the Son of Man is within you [cf. Luke 17: 21]. Follow him; those who seek him will find him [cf. Matt. 7: 7]. Go, therefore, and preach the Gospel of the Kingdom [cf. Matt. 4: 23; 9: 15; Mark 16: 15]. I have left no commandment but what I have commanded you, and I have given you no law, as the lawgiver did, lest you be bound by it."

When he had said this, he went away. But they were grieved and mourned greatly, saying, " How shall we go to the Gentiles and preach the Gospel of the Kingdom of the Son of Man? If even he was not spared, how shall we be spared? "*

Then Mary stood up and greeted all of them and said to her brethren, " Do not mourn or grieve or be irresolute, for his grace will be with you all and will defend you. Let us rather praise his greatness, for he prepared us and made us into men." When Mary said this, their hearts changed for the better, and they began to discuss the words of the [Saviour].

Peter said to Mary, " Sister, we know that the Saviour loved you more than other women [cf. John 11: 5, Luke 10: 38-42]. Tell us the words of the Saviour which you have in mind since you know them; and we do not, nor have we heard them."

Mary answered and said, " What is hidden from you I will impart to you." And she began to say the following words to them. " I," she said, " I saw the Lord in a vision and I said to him, ' Lord, I saw you to-day in a vision.' He answered and said to me, ' Blessed are you, since you did not waver at the sight of me. For where the mind is, there is your countenance ' [cf. Matt. 6:21]. I said to him, ' Lord, the mind which sees the vision, does it see it through the soul or through the spirit? ' The Saviour answered and said, ' It sees neither through the soul nor through the spirit, but the mind, which is between the two, which sees the vision, and it is. . .' "

* Or, " if they did not spare him, how will they spare us? " (Hardy).

[At this point pages 11-14 of the papyrus are lost.]

". . . and Desire said, 'I did not see you descend; but now I see you rising. Why do you speak falsely, when you belong to me?' The soul answered and said, 'I saw you, but you did not see me or recognise me; I served you as a garment and you did not recognise me.' After it had said this, it went joyfully and gladly away. Again it came to the third power, Ignorance. This power questioned the soul: 'Whither are you going? You were bound in wickedness, you were bound indeed.* Judge not' [cf. Matt. 7: 1]. And the soul said, 'Why do you judge me, when I judged not? I was bound, though I did not bind. I was not recognised,† but I recognised that all will go free, things both earthly and heavenly.' After the soul had left the third power behind,‡ it rose upward, and saw the fourth power, which had seven forms. The first form is darkness, the second desire, the third ignorance, the fourth the arousing§ of death, the fifth is the kingdom of the flesh, the sixth is the wisdom of the folly of the flesh, the seventh is wrathful [?] wisdom. These are the seven participants in‖ wrath. They ask the soul, 'Whence do you come, killer of men, or where are you going, conqueror of space?' The soul answered and said, 'What seizes me is killed; what turns me about is overcome; my desire has come to an end and ignorance is dead. In a world I was saved from a world, and in a "type," from a higher "type" and from the fetter of the impotence of knowledge, the existence of which is temporal. From this time I will reach rest in the time of the moment of the Aeon in silence.'"

When Mary had said this, she was silent, since the Saviour had spoken thus far with her. But Andrew answered and said

---

* Quite possibly dittography (H.).
† Or "they bound one, though I did not bind; they did not recognise me" (H.).
‡ Or "conquered the third power" (Till).
§ Or "jealousy" (H.).
‖ Or perhaps "powers of" (H.).

to the brethren, " Say what you think concerning what she said. For I do not believe that the Saviour said this. For certainly these teachings are of other ideas."

Peter also opposed her in regard to these matters and asked them about the Saviour. " Did he then speak secretly with a woman [cf. John 4: 27], in preference to us, and not openly? Are we to turn back and all listen to her? Did he prefer her to us? "

Then Mary grieved and said to Peter, " My brother Peter, what do you think? Do you think that I thought this up myself in my heart or that I am lying concerning the Saviour? "

Levi answered and said to Peter, " Peter, you are always irate. Now I see that you are contending against the woman like the adversaries. But if the Saviour made her worthy, who are you to reject her? Surely the Saviour knew her very well [cf. Luke 10: 38-42]. For this reason he loved her more than us [cf. John 11: 5]. And we should rather be ashamed and put on the Perfect Man, to form us [?] as he commanded us, and proclaim the gospel, without publishing a further commandment or a further law than the one which the Saviour spoke." When Levi had said this, they began to go out in order to proclaim him and preach him.

w. TILL, *Die gnostischen Schriften, 63-79.*

2

The Secret Book of John

This work occupies pages 19-77 of the Berlin Coptic papyrus. In W. Till's edition it has been collated with the version found in the first volume of the Gnostic library at Nag-Hammadi. The passages in Irenaeus based on the ' Apocryphon ' will be found in Part I, 12-13.

It happened one day when John, the brother of James (these are sons of Zebedee), went up to the temple [Acts 3 : 1], there a Pharisee named A [.] manaias approached him and said to him, " Where is your master whom you followed? " He said to him, " He has returned to the place from which he came." The Pharisee said to him, " This Nazarene deceived you with deception [. . . .] and hardened your hearts and estranged you from the tradition of your fathers."

When I [John] heard this, I went away from the temple to the mountain,* to a desert place, and with great grief in my heart I said, " How then was the Saviour appointed? And why was he sent into the world by his Father who sent him? And who is his Father? And what is the nature of that Aeon to which we shall go? He told us, ' This Aeon received the type of that imperishable Aeon,' but he did not reveal to us what its nature is."

As I had these thoughts the heavens were opened and the whole creation shone with a light [not of earth] and the universe was shaken. I was afraid and fell down, and behold, a child appeared to me; but I saw the form of an old man in

---

* Mount of Olives [Acts 1 : 12] (Till).

whom was light. When I looked upon him I did not comprehend this wonder. If it is a unity [?] with many forms because
of the light? Then its forms [appear] through their [. . . .].
If it is a unity, how would it have three aspects?

He said to me, " John, why do you doubt [cf. Matt. 28: 17]?
When I [. . . .] you? For it is not foreign to you. Do not be
of little faith; I am the one who is with you always [Matt.
28: 20]. I am [the Father], I am the Mother, I [am the Son].
I am the eternally Existent [Exodus 3: 14], the unmixable [for
there is no one] who mixed himself with him. Now I have
come to reveal to you that which is, that which has been, and
that which will be [cf. Rev. 1: 19], so that you may know the
things which are seen and the things not seen and to reveal to
you about the perfect Man [cf. Eph. 4: 13]. Now lift up your
face and come and hear and learn what I shall tell you to-day,
so that you yourself may reveal it to spirits of the same sort,
who are of the unwavering race of the Perfect Man and are
able to understand."

He said to me, " The Spirit [?] is a Unity, over which no
one rules. It is the God of Truth, the Father of the All, the
Holy Spirit, the invisible one, the one who is over the All, the
one who exists in his imperishability, the one who exists in
pure light into which no sight can look.

" One must not consider the Spirit as God or as of a
specific quality, for it is more excellent than the gods. It is
a Beginning that none precedes, for no one existed before it
and it has no need of them. It does not need life, for it is
eternal; it needs nothing, for it is not perfectible, since it has
no deficiency which might be perfected, but is beyond all perfection. It is light. It is illimitable because no one is before it
to give it limits; undifferentiated, because no one is before it
to differentiate it; immeasurable, because no one has measured
it as though existing before; invisible, because no one has seen
it [John 1: 18]. It is the eternal which always exists, the
indescribable because no one has apprehended it so as to
describe it, the one whose name no one can tell because no one
existed before it to name it.

" It is the immeasurable Light, the holy and pure purity, the indescribable, perfect and imperishable. It is not perfection or beatitude or deity, but something far more excellent. It is not boundless nor are limits set to it; it is something more excellent. It is neither corporeal nor incorporeal, not great, not small, not a quantity, not a creature; no one can think it. It is not anything existent, but something prior—not as if in itself it were prior, but because it is its own. It has no part in an Aeon. Time does not belong to it, for one which participates in an aeon has been formed by others. Time is not allotted to it, since it receives nothing from any other which allots. It makes use of nothing. In short, there is nothing before it. It seeks only itself in the perfection of Light, and comprehends the pure Light. The immeasurable greatness, the eternal, the giver of eternity, the Light, the giver of light, the life, the giver of life, the blessed one, the giver of blessedness, the knowledge, the giver of knowledge, the eternal good, the giver of good, the benefactor; that which is not of such a kind because it is such, but it gives [qualities]; the merciful mercy, the grace-giving grace, the immeasurable Light.

" What shall I say to you of It, the incomprehensible—the vision of the light—corresponding to what I shall be able to comprehend? for who will ever comprehend It as I can discuss It with you?

" Its Aeon is imperishable existing in rest and reposing in silence. It existed before the All. It is the head of all Aeons. If another were with It—for no one among us has recognised that which belongs to the immeasurable one except the one who dwelt in it. He told this to us [cf. John 1: 18], he who alone understands himself in his own light which surrounds him, he who is the fount of the water of life, the light full of purity.

" The fount of the Spirit flowed out of the living water of light [cf. John 7: 38]. And It supplied all Aeons and all worlds in every way. It understood Its own image, when It saw it in the pure water of light which surrounds It. And Its Thought became operative and revealed herself. She stood

before It out of the splendour of the light, which is the Power
which is before the All, the Power which has revealed itself
and is the perfect Forethought of the universe, the Light, the
copy of Light, the image of the invisible. She is the perfect
Power, the Barbelo, the perfect Aeon of glory. She praises It
because she appeared through It and understands It. She is
the First Thought, Its Image; she became a First Man, i.e.,
the Virginal Spirit, the thrice-male one, which has three
powers, three names, three acts of generation; the Aeon
which does not age, the male-female which came out of Its
Forethought.

" And Barbelo asked It to give her First Knowledge. It
consented, and when It had consented, First Knowledge
revealed herself and placed herself with Thought, i.e., Forethought, while they praised the Invisible One and the Perfect
Power, Barbelo, because they originated through her. And
again, First Knowledge asked this Power to give her Imperishability. And when It had consented, Imperishability revealed
herself and placed herself with Thought and First Knowledge,
while they praised the Invisible One and Barbelo, because it
was through her that they had originated. She asked that
Eternal Life might be given her. It consented, and when It
had consented, Eternal Life revealed herself, and they stood
there while they praised It and Barbelo, because it was through
her that they had originated in the revelation permitted by
the Invisible Spirit. This is the Five of the Aeons of the Father
—First Man [the image of the Invisible One, i.e., Barbelo]
and Thought and First Knowledge and Imperishability and
Eternal Life. This is the male-female Five, the tenth of the
Aeons, the Father of the ungenerated Father.

" Barbelo looked intensely into the pure Light and she
turned to It and gave birth to a blessed Spark of Light; but
he was not equal to her in greatness. This is the Monogenes,
who revealed himself to the Father, the divine Self-born, the
first-born Son of the All, from the Spirit of the pure Light.
And the Invisible Spirit rejoiced at the Light which came into
existence, which appeared through the First Power [Fore-

thought, Barbelo]. It anointed him with Its goodness so that he became perfect, faultless, and Christ [anointed] because It has anointed him with the goodness of the Invisible Spirit. He appeared before it and received anointing through the Virginal Spirit; and he stood before It while he praised the Invisible Spirit and the perfect Forethought, this Spirit in which he had dwelt. And he asked It to give him one thing only, Mind. The Invisible Spirit consented; Mind revealed itself and stood with Christ while they praised It and Barbelo. All these, however, came into existence in silence and a Thought. The Invisible Spirit willed to make something; its Will became corporeal; Will revealed itself and stood with Mind and the Light while it praised It. Logos followed Will, for through the Logos, Christ created all things. The divine Self-born, Eternal Life, and Will, and Mind and First Knowledge placed themselves while they praised the Invisible Spirit and Barbelo. For it was through her that they came into existence, and through the Spirit of the [divine?] eternal Self-born—son of Barbelo because he came to the eternal Virginal and Invisible Spirit—the Self-born God, Christ, whom the Spirit honoured with great honour because he came into existence from Its First Thought. The Invisible Spirit appointed him as God over the All [cf. Rom. 9: 5]. The true God gave him all power and subjected to him the Truth which was in it, so that he might comprehend the All. His name will be told to those who are worthy of him.

"But out of the Light, which is Christ, and out of Imperishability, through the working of the Invisible Spirit, the four great Lights revealed themselves from the divine Self-born, in order to place themselves by him and by the three. Will and Thought and Life. Now these four are Grace, Comprehension, Perception, and Prudence. Grace is at the first Light, Harmozel, which is the angel of light in the first Aeon; and there are three Aeons with it—Grace, Truth, and Form. At the second Light, Oroiael, which he has appointed over the second Aeon, there are three Aeons—Forethought, Perception, and Memory. At the third Light, Daueithe, which he has appointed

over the third Aeon, there are three Aeons—Comprehension,
Love, and Idea. At the fourth Light, Eleleth, which he has
appointed over the fourth Aeon, there are three Aeons—
Perfection, Peace, and Sophia. These are the four Lights
which stand by the Self-generator of the gods, the twelve
Aeons, which stand by the child, by the great Self-generator-
Christ, through the good pleasure of God, the Invisible Spirit.
The twelve Aeons belong to the Son, the Self-generated. All
things are made fast according to the will of the Holy Spirit
through the Self-born.

" Out of First Knowledge and perfect Mind, through God,
through the good pleasure of the great Invisible Spirit and
through the good pleasure of the Self-born, came forth the
perfect true Man, the first appearance. He called him Adam,
and appointed him over the first Aeon with the great God, the
Self-generator Christ, in the first Aeon of Harmozel; and his
powers are with him. And the Invisible Spirit gave him an
invincible, intelligible Power. The Man said, ' I glorify and
praise the Invisible Spirit, for because of thee all things came
into existence, and all things aspire to thee. But I praise thee
and the Self-born with the Aeons, the Three—the Father and
the Mother and the Son, the perfect Power.'

" And he appointed his son Seth over the second Light,
Oroiael. In the third Aeon was placed the seed of Seth, the
souls of the saints who are eternally in the third Light, Daueithe.
In the fourth Aeon were placed the souls who recognised their
perfection and did not immediately repent but persisted;
finally they repented. They will remain at the fourth Light,
Eleleth, which joined them with itself while they praise the
Invisible Spirit.

" Our sister Sophia, being an Aeon, conceived a thought
from herself. Thinking of the Spirit and of First Knowledge,
she willed to let a copy appear out of herself. The Spirit did
not agree with her or consent with her, nor did her Consort, the
male Virginal Spirit, approve. She found no more her supporter, when she consented without the good pleasure of the
spirit and the knowledge of her own supporter. Because of the

Desire [*Prunicon*] that was in her, she emanated outward. Her
thought could not remain unproductive, and her work came
forth, imperfect and ugly in appearance, because she had made
it without her Consort. It did not resemble its mother's appearance but was of another form. When she considered it she
saw that it was a copy of another appearance, since it had the
appearance of a snake and a lion. Its eyes were shining with
fire. She pushed it away from herself, outside those places, so
that none of the Immortals might see it, because she had
brought it to birth in ignorance; she joined a cloud of light
with it, and set a throne in the middle of the cloud, so that
no one might see it except the Holy Spirit, which is called
Life, the Mother of All. And she named it Ialdabaoth. This
is the First Archon. From his mother he drew great power,
and he withdrew from her and turned away from the place
where he was born. He took possession of another place; he
created for himself an Aeon, flaming with shining fire [cf. Gen.
3: 24], where he still is.

"And he joined himself with the Unreason which was
with him, and called the Powers into existence, twelve angels
under him, each in his Aeon according to the model of the
Imperishable Aeons. And for each of them he created seven
angels; and the angels with three powers, so that all those
under him are 360 angelic powers, including their three
powers, which correspond to the appearance of the first model
which was before him. When the Powers had revealed themselves from the arch-generator, the First Archon of the Darkness, from the Ignorance of the one who begot them, they
had the following names: the first is Iaoth, the second Hermas
[the eye of fire], the third Galila, the fourth Iobel, the fifth
Adonaios, the sixth Sabaoth, the seventh Kainan and Kae
[who is called Cain, which is the sun], the eighth Abiressine,
the ninth Iobel, the tenth Harmupiael, the eleventh Adonin,
the twelfth Belias.* They all have still other names because of
lust and wrath; they have still other double names which are
given them; these were given them because of the glory of the

* See page 95.

heaven. But these names correspond to the truth which reveals their nature. And Saclas called them by these names in a vision and in [relation to] their power. Through periods of time they withdraw and grow weak; through periods of time they obtain strength and grow powerful.

"And he ordained that seven kings rule over the heavens and five over the chaos of Hades [*amente*]. The names of glory of those who rule over the seven heavens are these; the first is Iaoth, with the face of a lion; the second Eloaios, with the face of an ass; the third Astaphaios, with the face of a hyena; the fourth Iao, with the face of a seven-headed snake; the fifth Adonaios, with the face of a dragon; the sixth Adoni, with the face of an ape; the seventh Sabbataios, with a face of shining flames of fire. This is the Seven of the week; these are the ones who govern the world.*

"But Ialdabaoth, Saclas, who possesses many forms in order to reveal himself with diverse forms as he pleases, apportioned to them some of his own fire and power. He did not give them any of the pure light which he had drawn from his Mother. Hence he governed them because of the glory which was in him from the power of the light of the Mother; hence he let himself be called God because he rebelled against the substance out of which he came into existence.

"And he joined seven powers with the Authorities. Because he spoke, they came into existence [Ps. 33: 9]; he gave them names, and appointed authorities. He began from above. The first is the Forethought with the first, Iaoth; the second is the Deity with the second, Eloaios; the third is the Goodness with the third, Astaphaios; the fourth is the Fire with the fourth, Iao; the fifth is the Kingdom with the fifth, Sabaoth; the sixth is the Comprehension with the sixth, Adonaios; the seventh is the Sophia with the seventh, Sabbataios. These have a firmament like heaven and an Aeon according to the Aeon-appearance which from the beginning existed after the model of the Imperishable Ones.

"He saw the creation beneath him, and the multitude of

* See page 57.

angels beneath him, who came into existence out of him, and he said to them, ' I am a jealous God; there is no other god beside me ' [Deut. 5: 9, Exod. 20: 3]—already indicating to the angels beneath him that another god does exist. For if there were no other, of whom would he be jealous? The Mother then began to be ' borne about ' [Gen. 1: 2] because she recognised her deficiency. Because her consort had not agreed with her, she had diminished in her perfection."

I said, " Christ, what does ' borne about ' mean? " He smiled and said, " Do you think it is, as Moses said, ' above the waters '? Not at all. She saw the wickedness and the apostasy which clung to her son. She repented, and while she went to and fro in the darkness of ignorance, she began to be ashamed and did not venture to return [above] but went to and fro. This going to and fro is ' to be borne about.' After the self-satisfied one had received a power from the Mother, he did not know many things which were set over his Mother. He thought that his Mother alone existed. He saw the countless army of angels which he had made, and he felt himself exalted above them. But when the Mother knew that the abortion of darkness was imperfect, since her consort had not agreed with her, she repented and grieved exceedingly. He heard the prayer of her repentance and the brothers petitioned on her behalf. The Holy Invisible Spirit gave permission, and after the Holy Invisible Spirit had given permission, It poured over her a spirit from the Perfection. Her consort came down to her in order to correct her deficiency. He decided in his forethought to correct her deficiency. She was not led back to her own Aeon, but because of the abundant ignorance which had appeared in her, she is in the Nine until she corrects her deficiency.

" A voice came to her: ' Man exists, and the Son of Man.' The first Archon Ialdabaoth heard it, and he thought that the voice had not come down. [. . . .] To him the holy, perfect Father, the First Man in the form of a man. The Blessed One revealed his appearance to them, and the whole archontic group of the seven Authorities gave permission. They saw in

the water the appearance of the image, and they said to one
another, ' Let us make a man, after the image and after the
appearance of God ' [cf. Gen. 1 : 26]. From one another they
created, and from all their powers they formed a formation
from themselves. And each one of every power in his power
created the soul. They created it after the image which they
had seen, by way of an imitation of Him who was from the
beginning, the Perfect Man. They said, ' Let us call him
Adam, so that the name of this being and his power may
become a light for us.' And the powers began from below.
The first is Deity, i.e., a soul of bone; the second is Goodness,
i.e., the desire [?] of the soul; the third is Fire, i.e., a flesh-
soul; the fourth is Providence, i.e., a marrow-soul, and the
whole framing of the body; the fifth is Kingdom, i.e., a blood-
soul; the sixth is Understanding, i.e., a head-soul; the seventh
is Sophia, i.e., a hair-soul. And they set the whole body in
order, and their angels came to them [from the number (?)]
of those who were first prepared by the Authorities, the Soul-
substances, for the arrangement of the joined members. And
they made the whole body, fitted together from the army of
angels, whom I have already mentioned. And it remained
inert for a long time, since the seven Authorities could not
raise it up, nor could the 360 angels who assembled [the
members].

"And the Mother wanted to recover the power which
she had given to the Archon of Prunicos. She came in innocence
and prayed to the Father of All, the one rich in mercy, the
God of Light. By a holy decree he sent the Self-born and the
Four Lights in the form of the angels of the First Archon. They
advised him so that they might bring forth the power of the
Mother from him. They said to him, " Breathe in his face
[something] of the spirit which is in you, and the object will
raise itself up." So he breathed into him some of his spirit—
i.e., the power of the Mother—into the body, and he moved.
And the other powers were jealous because he originated
from them all, and they had given the man the powers which
were derived from them, and he had taken to himself the souls

of the seven Authorities and their powers. His wisdom was stronger than all of them, stronger than the First Archon. And they knew that he was free from wickedness, since he was more intelligent than they were, and had come in the Light. They took him and brought him down to the region at the bottom of all matter.

" But the blessed Father is a compassionate benefactor. He took pity on the power of the Mother which had been taken from the First Archon so that it might obtain power over the body. He sent out the good Spirit [he and his great compassion] as a helper for the first one who had come down, who was called Adam—namely, the Thought of Light, which by him was called ' Life.'* This is she who works at the whole creature [Adam] since she labours with the creature [cf. Rom. 8: 22], sets him in his own perfect temple, explains the coming down of his flaw, and shows him his way upwards. And the Thought of Light was hidden in him so that the Archons would not perceive it but our sister [Sophia . . . .] might correct her error through the Thought of Light. And the man shone forth because of the shadow of the Light which is in him, and his thinking rose higher than those who had created him. And they agreed and saw that the man had raised himself above them. They made a resolution with the whole angelic array of the Archons and with the rest of their powers. Then fire and earth united with water and flame. They were confounded with the four winds, so that they blew fierily, united one with another, and caused a great commotion. They brought [him] into the shadow of death.

" Then they made another formation out of earth, water, fire, and wind; i.e., out of matter, darkness, desire, and the Opposed Spirit. This is the fetter, this is the tomb of the formation, of the body, which was put on man as the fetter of matter. This is the first one who came down, and his first separation. But the Thought of Light is in him and awakens his thought.

The First Archon brought him and placed him in paradise,

* Eve the " helper " of Adam in Gen. 2: 18 (cf. 3:20).

of which he said that it would be a 'delight' for him; that means that he tricked him. For their delight is bitter and their beauty is lawless. Their delight is deceit and their tree was hostility. Their fruit is poison, against which there is no healing, and their promise is death for him. Their tree was planted as the 'tree of life.' But I will proclaim to you the mystery of their life; that is their Imitation Spirit, which comes from them, so that it will lead him astray, so that he will not know his perfection. That tree is made as follows: its root is bitter; its branches are shadows of death; its leaves are hate and deceit; its sap is an ointment of wickedness and its fruit is the desire of death; its seed drinks up those who taste it; the Hades [*amente*] is their abode.

"But the tree which they call 'of the knowledge of good and evil,' this is the Thought of Light, on whose account the commandment was given not to taste of it, that is, 'do not hear them,' since the commandment was directed against him, so that he might not look up towards his perfection nor know his nakedness in relation to his perfection. But I have brought you to eat of it."

I said to him, "Christ, was it not the serpent who taught her?"

He smiled and said, "The serpent taught her the begetting of desire for pollution and corruption, since these serve him. And he knew that she would not obey him, since she is shrewder than he. He wanted to bring out the power which had been given him by him, and he let lack of perception settle upon Adam."

I said to him, "Christ, what is lack of perception?"

He said, "It is not as Moses said, 'He let him sleep' [Gen. 2:21], but he enveloped his senses with a veil and burdened him with anesthesia. For he said through the prophet [Isaiah 6:10], 'I will harden the ears of your hearts so that you may not understand and may not see.' Then the Thought of Light hid herself in him and in his will he decided to bring her forth out of the rib. But the Thought of Light, since she is unattainable, even though Darkness pursued her,

it could not grasp her [cf. John 1 : 5]. He decided to bring
the power out of him and again make a formation with a
female form. And he let it arise before him; not as Moses
said, ' He took a rib and created the woman for him ' [Gen.
2 : 21-22]. Immediately he became sober from the intoxication
of the Darkness. The Thought of Light removed the veil from
his mind; and as he recognised [in her] his essence, he said,
' This is now bone of my bones and flesh of my flesh ' [Gen.
2 : 23]. For this reason the man will leave his father and his
mother and will cleave to his wife and the two will become
one flesh [Gen. 2 : 24]. Because they will send the consort of
the Mother, and will raise her up, because of this Adam called
her ' Mother of all living ' [Gen. 3 : 20].

" From the Absolute Sovereignty [*authentia*] of the Height
and of revelation, Thought taught them knowledge through
the tree, in the form of an eagle: She taught them to eat
knowledge so that he might take care of his perfection, since
both had the flaw [a word also meaning " corpse "] of ignorance. Ialdabaoth knew that they withdrew from him. He
cursed them, and furthermore ordained that the man should
be lord over the woman, though he [Ialdabaoth] was ignorant
of the mystery [Eph. 5 : 32] which originated from the decree
of the holy Height.

" But they [Adam and Eve] were afraid to curse him and to
uncover his ignorance. All his angels drove them out of
Paradise and he surrounded it with thick darkness. Then
Ialdabaoth saw the virgin who stood beside Adam. Senseless-
ness filled him [Ialdabaoth] and he wanted to let a seed sprout
from her. He seduced her [Eve] and begot the first son, and
similarly the second: Yahweh, with a face like a bear, and
Elohim, with a face like a cat. But one is righteous, while the
other is unrighteous. Elohim is the righteous, Yahweh the
unrighteous. He set the righteous one over fire and wind; the
unrighteous one he set over water and earth. These are the
ones who up to the present day are called Cain and Abel
among all generations of men. Marital intercourse arose
through the First Archon. He planted in Adam a desire for

sowing, so that it is of this essence that women produce a copy
from their Imitation [Spirit]. And he set the two Archons
over the principalities, so that they might rule over the grave
[i.e., body].

"Adam knew his nature and begot Seth [Gen. 4: 25].
And as in the generation which is in heaven under the Aeons,
so the Mother sent the [Spirit] which belongs to her. The
Spirit descended to her in order to awaken the nature which
is like it, after the model of perfection, in order to awaken
them from lack of perception and from the wickedness of the
grave. So it remained for a time and worked for the seed, so
that when the Spirit comes from the holy Aeons it may place
them outside deficiency in the arrangement of the Aeon; so
that it may become holy perfection, so that deficiency may no
longer be with it."

And I said, " Christ, will the souls all live longer than the
purity of light? "

He said to me, " You have come to a perception of great
things, which are hard to reveal to others than those who are
of the generation which does not waver. Those upon whom
the Spirit of Life descends, when they are bound together with
the power, will be saved and will become perfect and they
will become worthy to rise upward to that great light; for they
will become worthy to purify themselves with them from every
evil and from the temptations of wickedness, so that they no
longer direct their glance at anything but the imperishable
assembly, and strive for it without anger, envy, fear, desire, and
satiety. They will be affected by none of these except only the
flesh, which they use while they wait to be led forth and
received by the Receiver into the honour of eternal, imperishable life and their vocation, in which they endure all things
and suffer all things [1 Cor. 13: 7] so that they may pass
through the struggle and inherit eternal life."

I said, " Christ, if they have not done this, what will the
souls into which the power and the Spirit of Life have entered,
do so that they too may be saved? "

He said to me " The souls to which that Spirit comes will

under all circumstances live, and they come out of evil. For the power enters all men; without it they cannot stand [upright]. But after it [the soul] is born, then the Spirit of Life will be brought to it. And when it comes this strong, divine Spirit to the life, it strengthens the power—i.e., the soul—and it does not turn aside to wickedness. But in the case of those whom the Imitation Spirit enters, it leads it [the soul] astray and it [the soul] errs."

I said, " Christ, the souls of these, when they come out of the flesh, whither will they go? "

He smiled and said, " To a place for the soul, i.e., the power which is far superior to the Imitation Spirit. This is strong; it escapes from the works of wickedness and through the imperishable guidance it will be saved and raised up to the Rest of the Aeons."

I said, " Christ, those who have not known the All, what are their souls or whither will they go? "

He said to me, " An Imitation Spirit has overgrown them in their stumbling, and so the Imitation Spirit burdens their souls, draws it [the soul] to the works of wickedness, and brings it in this way to lack of perception. After the soul is unclothed, it [the Imitation Spirit] delivers it to the powers which are under the Archon. They [the souls] will once more be cast into fetters and led about until they are saved from lack of perception, attain knowledge, and so will be perfected and saved."

I said, " Christ, how then does the soul gradually shrivel up and return into the nature of the Mother or of the Man? "

He rejoiced when I asked him, and he said, " Blessed are you for a clear understanding [*parakolouthesis*]. Therefore they will be given together with the other in whom the Spirit of Life is a consequence [*akolouthesis*] for him.* And because it [the soul] hears through him, it will be saved. It no longer goes into another flesh."

I said to him, " Christ, those who have known but have turned away, what are their souls? "

* Christ? Inner man?

He said to me, " They will go to the place where the angels of impoverishment [cf. Gal. 4: 9] will withdraw, for whom there is no portion of repentance [cf. Heb. 12: 17]. They will all be preserved for the day on which they will be punished. All who have blasphemed against the Holy Spirit [Matt. 12: 31] will be tormented in eternal punishment " [cf. Heb. 6: 4-8].

I said, " Christ, whence came the Imitation Spirit? "

He said to me, " When the merciful Mother and the Holy Spirit, the merciful, which troubled itself with us—that is, the Thought of Light—and the seed which it awakened in the thought of the men of the generation of this perfect and eternal man of light—then the First Archon recognised that she surpassed him in the height of their wisdom. He wanted to get possession of their counsel. Since he is ignorant,* he did not know that they are wiser than he is. He took counsel with his powers. They brought Fate into being and through measure, periods, and seasons they imprisoned the gods of the heavens, the angels, the demons, and men, so that all would come into its fetters and it [Fate] would be lord over all: an evil and tortuous plan. And he repented for everything which had come into being through him [cf. Gen. 6: 6]. He decided to let a flood come over the whole presumption of men. And the greatness of Providence, i.e., the Thought of Light, informed Noah. He made a proclamation to men, yet they did not believe him. Not as Moses said, ' He hid himself in an ark ' [cf. Gen. 7: 16], but he covered himself in a Place. Not only Noah, but other people from the generation which does not waver, went to a Place and covered themselves with a cloud of light. And he recognised the authority from above, together with those who were with him in the light which shone on them; for the darkness was poured out over everything on the earth.

" He took counsel with his angels; they sent their angels to the daughters of men, so that they might let seed generate

* On the following passage cf. H. C. Puech, *Gnosis and Time, Man and Time* (Papers from the Eranos Yearbooks, III, New York, 1957), 71-72.

from them for their pleasure. At first they had no success. They all came to a decision to create the Imitation Spirit, so that they might remember the Spirit which came down. And the angels changed their forms into the appearance of their husbands and they sowed with the spirit which tormented them in the darkness. Out of wickedness they brought them gold, silver, gifts and the metals; copper and iron and all sorts, and they led them into temptation so that they would not remember their Providence, which does not waver.* And they took them and begot children [cf. Gen. 6: 1] out of the darkness through their Imitation Spirit. Their hearts were hardened, they became hard through the hardening of the Imitation Spirit, even until now.

" The One to be praised, the Father-Mother, the One rich in mercy, takes form in her [its] seed.

" I first came up [or down] to the perfect Aeon.

" I say this to you, so that you may write it down and give it in secret to your fellow spirits. For this mystery belongs to the generation which does not waver.

" The Mother once descended before me. But these are the things which she effected in the world; she raised up her seed.

" I will proclaim to you what will take place; and indeed I have given you this, so that you may write it down, and it will certainly be deposited."

Then he said to me, " Cursed is anyone who exchanges this for a gift or for food or drink or clothing or anything else of the sort."

He gave him [John] this mystery and forthwith disappeared from him. And he [John] came to his fellow disciples and began to tell them what had been said to him by the Saviour.

W. TILL, *Die gnostischen Schriften, 78-195.*

* Cf. I Enoch, 7-8.

PART III

MINOR DOCUMENTS OF THE SECOND AND THIRD CENTURIES

This section includes documents describing diagrams used by the Ophites; the remains of the book 'Baruch' by the Gnostic Justin; a late Marcionite system which seems to have been influenced by 'Baruch'; examples of Naassene exegesis; and the 'Hymn of the Soul' to be found in the apocryphal 'Acts of Thomas.'

The Ophite Diagrams

In his ' True Account,' an attack on Christianity written between 177 and 180, a certain Celsus described a diagram apparently used by Ophites (whom he regarded as genuine Christians). Seventy years later, in his reply to Celsus, the Christian theologian Origen provided a fuller description of a similar diagram. Both descriptions are to be found in Origen, 'Contra Celsum,' vi. 24-38. The present translation has been revised in the light of that made by Henry Chadwick (' Origen Contra Celsum,' Cambridge, 1953).

Discussions of the diagrams will be found in T. Hopfner, " Das Diagram der Ophiten," ' Charisteria Rzach ' (Reichenberg, 1930), 86-98, and G. Bornkamm, " Ophiten," Pauly-Wissowa, ' Real-Encyclopädie der classischen Altertumswissenschaft,' XVIII, 1, 654-58.

A. CELSUS' DESCRIPTION

Celsus says there is a diagram consisting of ten [or seven] separate circles, circumscribed by one circle which is said to be the world-soul and is called Leviathan. The diagram is divided by a thick black line, which is called Gehenna, i.e., Tartarus. The " seal " is that of the one who imposes it, who is called Father; the one sealed is called Youth and Son, and he responds: " I have been anointed with white chrism from the tree of life." There are seven angels, who delivered the seal; they stand on both sides of the soul set free from the body; and there are other angels of light who are called Archontics. The Archon of the so-called Archontics is the accursed god of the Jews, who makes rain and thunder. He is the Demiurge of this world, the god of Moses described in his creation narrative. Of the seven archontic demons, the first is lion-shaped; the second is a bull; the third is amphibious and hisses horribly; the fourth has the form of an eagle; the fifth has the appearance of a bear; the sixth, that of a dog; and the seventh, that of an ass [it is named Thaphabaoth or Onoel]. Some persons return to the archontic forms so that they become lions or bulls or serpents or eagles or bears or dogs. There is a square, and there are words said at the gates of paradise.

They add still further matters: the sayings of prophets, and circles upon circles, and emanations of the earthly church and of circumcision, and the power emanating from a certain virgin Prunicos, and a living soul, and a heaven slain that it may live, and earth slain with a sword, and many slain that they may live, and death stopped in heaven, when the world's sin dies, and a narrow way back, and doors opening automatically. Everywhere there is the tree of life and a resurrection of flesh from the tree.

They say that some things are written within the two super-heavenly circles, the greater and lesser, those of the Son and the Father.

ORIGEN, *Contra Celsum* vi. 24-38.

B. ORIGEN'S DESCRIPTION

The first angel [lion-shaped] is called Michael; the second [bull-shaped] is called Souriel; the third [serpent-shaped] is called Raphael; the fourth [eagle-shaped] is called Gabriel; the fifth [bear-shaped] is called Thauthabaoth; the sixth [dog-shaped] is called Erathaoth; the seventh [ass-shaped] is called Onoel or Thartharaoth.

They are taught to say, after passing through the barrier

of evil, " I hail you, solitary King, Bond of invisibility, unin-
vestigated Forgetfulness, First Power, guarded by the spirit of
Foreknowledge and by Wisdom. From this place I am sent
on pure, already a part of the light of Son and Father. Let
Grace be with me, yes, Father, let it be with me." The beginning of the Eight is at that point. When they pass through
Ialdabaoth, they are to say, " O Ialdabaoth, you who have
come first and seventh to rule with confidence, ruling Reason
of pure Mind, perfect work of Son and Father: I bear a symbol
marked with the imprint of life and have opened to the world
the gate which you closed for your eternity: I am free again
and I pass your authority; let Grace be with me, yes, Father,
let it be with me." When they have passed through Ialdabaoth
and have come to Iao, they are to say, " You second Archon
of the hidden mysteries of Son and Father, night-shining Iao,
first master of Death, part of the blameless, bearing your beard
as a symbol; I am ready to pass by your rule. By the living
word I have overpowered him who came from you; let Grace
be with me, Father, let it be with me." To Sabaoth they are
to say, " Archon of the fifth authority, mighty Sabaoth,
guardian of the law of your creation which is destroyed by
grace, the more powerful Pentad, be with me as I see the
unassailable symbol of your art, preserved in the image of an
example, a body destroyed by the Pentad; let Grace be with
me, Father, let it be with me." Then to Astaphaeus they are
to say, " Astaphaeus, Archon of the third gate, overseer of the
first beginning of water, behold an initiate and be with me,
since I have been cleansed by a virginal Spirit; behold the
substance of the universe; let Grace be with me, Father, let
it be with me." After him is Aeloaeus, to whom they are to
say, " Aeloaeus, Archon of the second gate, be with me, since
I bear your mother's symbol, the Grace hidden from the
powers of authorities; let Grace be with me, Father, let it be
with me." Finally, they are to say to Horaeus, " You who
have fearlessly passed beyond the barrier of fire, Horaeus, you
who hold the power of the first gate, be with me since you see
the symbol of your power, a symbol destroyed by the example

of the tree of life and abandoned by the image after the likeness of the blameless one. Let Grace be with me, Father, let it be with me."*

In this diagram are the greater and the smaller circle. On their diameters is inscribed " Father " and " Son." Between the greater [in which the smaller lies] and another circle [consisting of two circles, the outer yellow and the inner dark blue] is the barrier, shaped like a two-edged axe. Above it is a small circle, smaller than the larger of those already mentioned, with " love " written on it. Below it is another with the word " life." In the second circle, combining and circumscribing the other two circles as well as another rhomboid shape, is written " Foreknowledge of Wisdom," and above their common intersection is a circle on which is written " Knowledge," and below, another in which is written " Understanding."

ORIGEN, *Contra Celsum,* vi. 24-38.

* See pages 192-4.

2

Baruch by Justin

All we know of Justin's system is contained in Hippolytus' ' Refutation of All Heresies,' though it seems to be reflected in a late Marcionite system described by Eznik (Ch. 3). In this system the universe owes its origin to three principles. The first is the only Good, at one point identified with the cosmic Priapus; the second and third are Elohim and Eden, or the Demiurge and matter. From the union of Elohim and Eden are derived the world-making angels and thence the world. To the first human couple is given the primary law to " increase and multiply." Evil is the violation of this law. It originates when Elohim ascends to contemplate his creation and is captivated by the Good. In her frustration, Eden ordered her angels to bring about violations of the primary law, in order to torment Elohim's spirit within mankind. She worked especially through her angel Naas, the serpent in the garden. On the other hand, Elohim has sent his own angel Baruch [" blessed "] to contend with Naas and to gain adherents for himself. Baruch came to Adam and Eve, to Moses, to the prophets, to Heracles, and finally to Jesus. Only Jesus remained faithful to Baruch and ascended to the Good.

This system is a combination of a philosophical or theological triad, common in second-century thought, with a psychological, almost Freudian, explanation of human and cosmic sin. Sin is violation of the propagation of the human species; it originates in frustration and results in frustration. Salvation comes through returning to the Good, the life-principle, Priapus.

See E. Haenchen, " Das Buch Baruch," ' Zeitschrift für Theologie und Kirche,' *50 (1953), 123-58;* R. M. Grant, " Gnosis Revisited," ' Church History ' *23 (1954),* 36-45; G. Salmon in ' Dictionary of Christian Biography ' III (London, 1882), 587-89.

[The Oath of Secrecy.] If you wish to know " what eye has not seen or ear heard, and what has not entered the heart of man " [1 Cor. 2: 9], the One who is high above all good things, swear to keep secret the mysteries of the teaching; for our Father, having seen the Good and having been made perfect with him, kept secret the mysteries of silence, and he swore, as it is written, " The Lord swore and will not change his mind " [Ps. 110: 4]. This is the oath: " I swear by the One above all, the Good, to keep these mysteries and to tell them to no one and not to return from the Good to the creation." When he takes this oath, he enters in to the Good and sees " what eye has not seen or ear heard and what has not entered the heart of man," and he drinks from the living water, which is the washing, the spring of living water welling up [John 4: 10, 14]. For there was a division between water and water [Gen. 1: 6], and the water below the firmament belongs to the evil creation; in it are washed the earthly and psychical men. The water above the firmament belongs to the Good and is living; in it are washed the spiritual and living men, as Elohim was, when after washing he did not change his mind.

HIPPOLYTUS, *Ref.* v. 24.1; 37. 1-3

[The Myth.] There were three unbegotten principles of the universe, two male, one female. One of the male principles is called Good (the only one so called [Luke 18: 19]), who takes forethought for the universe; the other is called Father of all begotten beings, without foreknowledge, without knowledge, invisible. The female one is without foreknowledge, wrathful, double-minded, double-bodied, a virgin above and a viper below. She is called Eden and Israel. These are the principles of the universe, the roots and springs from which everything came; there was nothing else.

When the Father, without foreknowledge, saw that half-virgin Eden, he came to a desire for her [this Father is called Elohim]; Eden desired Elohim no less, and desire brought them into a single union of love. From such a union the father begot twelve angels for himself by Eden. The names of the paternal angels are these: Michael, Amen, Baruch, Gabriel, Esaddaeus . . . [seven names lost]. And similarly the names of the maternal angels which Eden made are listed; they are these: Babel, Achamoth, Naas, Bel, Belias, Satan, Sael, Adonaios, Kauithan, Pharaoth, Karkamenos, Lathen. Of these twenty-four angels the paternal ones side with the Father and act entirely according to his will, the maternal ones with the mother, Eden. The total of all the angels together in paradise, concerning which Moses says, " God planted paradise in Eden to the east " [Gen. 2: 8], that is, before the face of Eden, so that Eden might always see paradise, that is, the angels. The angels of this paradise are allegorically called trees, and the tree of life is the third of the paternal angels, Baruch, while the tree of the knowledge of good and evil is the third of the material angels, Naas. Moses spoke these things covertly because not all hold the truth [cf. Matt. 19: 11].

After paradise came into existence from the mutual satis-faction of Elohim and Eden, the angels of Elohim took some of the most excellent earth [that is, not from the bestial part of Eden but from the upper, anthropoid parts, the civilised regions of earth] and made man [cf. Gen. 2: 7]. From the bestial parts came wild beasts and the other animals. They made man, then, as a symbol of their unity and love and they gave him shares of their own powers; Eden provided the soul and Elohim the spirit. And man, the Adam, became a kind of seal and memorial of their love and an eternal symbol of the marriage of Eden and Elohim. Similarly, as it was written by Moses, Eve became an image and a symbol, a seal of Eden to be kept for ever; and similarly the soul was set in the image Eve by Eden and the spirit by Elohim. And com-mandments were given them: " Increase and multiply and inherit the earth " [that is, Eden]. For Eden contributed all her power to Elohim, like a dowry in marriage. Therefore in imitation of that first marriage to this very day women present dowries to their husbands, in obedience to that divine and hereditary law which Eden obeyed in regard to Elohim.

When everything had been created, as it was written in the book of Moses, heaven and earth and the things in them, the twelve angels of the mother were divided " into four principles " [Gen. 2: 10], and each quadrant of these is called a river, Phison, Geon, Tigris, and Euphrates, as Moses says. These twelve angels, closely embraced in four parts, circle around and govern the universe, having a satrapic authority over the world derived from Eden.   They do not always remain in the same places, but circle around as in a circular chorus, changing from place to place and at various times and intervals giving up the places assigned them.   When Phison is in control of places, then famine, distress, and tribulation occurs in that part of the earth; for the injunction of these angels is niggardly [*pheidolon*].   Similarly there are evil times and formations of diseases in each part of the four in accordance with the power and nature of each.   This torrent of evil, in accordance with the rivers, that is, the control of the various quadrants, circles ceaselessly around the universe by the wish of Eden.

The necessity of evil is due to this cause.   When Elohim had fashioned and framed the universe out of mutual satisfaction, he wished to ascend to the highest parts of heaven and to see if anything was lacking in the creation.   He took his own angels with him, for he was by nature borne upwards.   He left Eden below, for being earth, she did not wish to follow her husband upwards.   When Elohim came to the upper limit of heaven and saw a light greater than the one he had fashioned, he said, " Open the gates for me so that I may enter and acknowledge the Lord [Ps. 118: 19]; for I thought that I was the Lord."   A voice from the light was given him; it said, " This is the gate of the Lord; the just enter through it " [Ps. 118: 20]. The gate was immediately opened, and the Father—without his angels—went in to the Good and saw

" what eye has not seen or ear heard, and what has not entered the heart of man." Then the Good said to him, " Sit at my right hand " [Ps. 110: 1]. The Father said to the Good, " Lord, let me destroy the universe which I made; for my spirit is imprisoned among men and I wish to take it back " [cf. Gen. 6: 3]. Then the Good said to him, " Nothing which comes from me can be evil; you and Eden made the universe from mutual satisfaction; let Eden have the creation as long as she wants it; you stay with me " [cf. John 21: 22]. Then Eden, knowing that she had been abandoned by Elohim, in grief set her angels about her and adorned herself attractively [cf. Gen. 2: 1], so that somehow Elohim might come to desire her and return to her. Under the control of the Good, however, Elohim no longer descended to Eden. Then Eden commanded Babel [Aphrodite] to fashion adulteries and divorces among men, so that just as she herself was separated from Elohim, so the spirit of Elohim in men might be grieved and tormented and experience the same sufferings as did the abandoned Eden. And Eden gave great authority to her third angel, Naas, so that he could torture the spirit of Elohim in men with all possible torments, and so that through the spirit Elohim might be tortured, he who had abandoned his wife in violation of the covenant he had made with his wife.

When the Father Elohim saw these things he sent forth Baruch, his own third angel, to help the spirit which is in all men. When Baruch came he stood in the midst of the angels of Eden, that is, in the midst of paradise [Gen. 2: 9]—paradise means the angels, in whose midst he stood—and commanded men " to eat from every tree in paradise, but not to eat from that of the knowledge of good and evil " [Gen. 2: 16-17]. This tree is Naas. He could obey the other eleven angels of Eden, for they have passions but not transgression of the commandment; Naas had transgression, for he approached Eve and seduced her and debauched her [and this is a transgression], and he also approached Adam and used him as a boy [and this is a transgression]; this was the origin of adultery and pederasty. From this time evil and good things have ruled over men. They originated from a single source, for when the Father ascended to the Good he showed the way for those who wish to ascend, and by departing from Eden he made the origin of evils for the spirit of the Father in men.

Baruch was sent to Moses, and through him spoke to the sons of Israel so that they would return to the Good; but the third [angel of Eden, Naas], through the soul given by Eden and dwelling in Moses, as in all men, overshadowed the commandments of Baruch and made his own commandments heard. For this reason the soul was set against the spirit and the spirit against the soul. For the soul is Eden, while the spirit is Elohim; and each is in all, both female and male.

After that Baruch was sent again to the prophets, so that through the prophets the spirit dwelling in men might hear and flee from Eden and the evil creation as the Father Elohim fled. And similarly by the same idea, through the soul dwelling in man with the spirit of the Father, Naas beguiled the prophets, and they were all beguiled and did not follow the words of Baruch, which Elohim commanded.

Finally Elohim chose a prophet from the uncircumcision, Heracles, and sent him to contend with the twelve angels of Eden and to free the [spirit of the] Father from the twelve evil angels of the creation. These are the twelve labours of Heracles in which Heracles contended in order, from the first to the last, the lion and the hydra and the boar and the rest; for these are the names of the nations which they were given from the power of the maternal angels. As he seemed to have been victorious, Omphale [Babel-Aphrodite] attacked him and seduced him and took off his power, the commandments of Baruch which Elohim commanded, and put on him her own robe, the power of Eden, which is the power from below. Thus the prophecy of Heracles and his works became ineffectual.

Finally " in the days of king Herod " [Luke 1: 5] Baruch was sent again by Elohim, and he came to Nazareth [Luke 1: 26] and found Jesus, the son of Joseph and Mary, feeding sheep, a boy of twelve years [Luke 2: 42], and he told him everything which had taken place from the beginning, from

Eden and Elohim and everything which will take place after this. He said, " All the prophets before you were seduced; but, Jesus, son of man, try not to be seduced but proclaim this message to men and tell them about the Father and about the Good and ascend to the Good and sit there with Elohim, the Father of us all." And Jesus obeyed the angel; he said, " Lord, I will do all things," and he made the proclamation. Naas wished to seduce him too, [but he was not able to do so], for Jesus remained faithful to Baruch. Then Naas became angry because he could not seduce him, and had him crucified. He left his body to Eden by the tree and ascended to the Good. For he said to Eden, " Woman, you have your son " [John 19: 26], that is, the psychical and earthly man, but he was " placing in the hands " the spirit of the Father [cf. Luke 23: 46], ascended to the Good.

The Good is Priapus, who created before there was anything [*prin-poiesas*];* he is called Priapus because he prefabricated everything. For this reason he is erected in every temple, is honoured by all creation, and before him on the roads carries fruits, that is, the fruits of creation, of which he was the cause, prefabricating the creation before there was any.†

Therefore, when you hear men say that the swan came upon Leda and produced offspring from her, the swan is Elohim and Leda is Eden. When men say that the eagle came upon Ganymede, the eagle is Naas and Ganymede is Adam. And when they say that the gold came upon Danae and brought forth a child from her, the gold is Elohim and Danae is Eden.

When the prophets say, " Hear, heaven, and give ear, earth; the Lord has spoken " [Is. 1: 2], heaven means the spirit of Elohim in men, earth the soul in man with the spirit, the Lord Baruch, Israel Eden; for the wife of Elohim is called Eden and Israel. " Israel did not know me " [Is. 1: 3]; for if it had known that I am with the Good, it would not have

---

* This etymology is apparently unique; cf. H. Herter, *De Priapo* (Giessen, 1932), 44.
† Cf. Cornutus, *Epidrome* 27, pp. 50-51 Lang.

tortured the spirit which is in men because of the Father's ignorance.

When the prophet says " to take for himself a woman of fornication because the earth has fornicated from behind the Lord " [Hos. 1 : 2], that is, Eden from Elohim, in these words the prophet clearly expressed the whole mystery, but he was not heard because of the wickedness of Naas.

HIPPOLYTUS, *Ref.* v. 26. 1-37; 27. 4.

3

Eznik's Résumé of Marcionite Doctrine

Marcion, in error, introduces a stranger as opposed to the god of the law, setting alongside him Hyle as a substance, and three heavens. In the first, they say, dwells the stranger; and in the second, the god of the law; and in the third, his armies; and on earth, Hyle, and they call her the power of the earth.

And so he disposes the world and the creatures, as the law says. But he adds also that in conjunction with Hyle god made all that he made and Hyle was, as it were, a female and a marriageable woman. And after making the world [god] himself rose with his armies to heaven: and Hyle and her sons remained on earth, and they each took dominion, Hyle on earth and the god of the law in heaven.

And having seen that the world was beautiful, the god of the law thought to make man upon it. And descending to earth unto Hyle, he said, " Give me of thy clay and I give spirit from myself and let us make man in our image." When Hyle had given him of her earth, he shaped it and breathed spirit into it, and Adam became a living soul and for that cause was he named Adam, because he was made of clay. And having shaped him and his wife, and having placed them in the garden, as the law also says, they came continually and commanded him and took pleasure in him as in a joint son.

And [Marcion] says, the god of the law, who was the lord of the world, seeing that Adam is noble and worthy for service, reflected how he could steal him from Hyle and attach him to his own side. Taking him aside, he said, 'Adam, I am god, and there is none other, and beside me thou shalt have none other god; but if thou hast another god beside me, thou shalt surely die." And when he had said this to him and had mentioned the name of death, Adam, terror-stricken, began to withdraw himself little by little from Hyle.

And when Hyle came to command him according to custom, she saw that Adam was not hearkening to her but, reflecting, kept himself apart and did not approach her. Then with astonishment in her heart Hyle realised that the lord of creatures had defrauded her. She said, " From the source of the fount is its water polluted. What is this? Adam is not increased yet with offspring and [god] has stolen him from me by means of the name of his deity. Since he hates me and has not kept the agreement with me, I shall make many gods and fill the whole world with them, that he may seek who is god and [god] will not be found."

And she made, they say, many idols and called them gods and filled the world with them. And the name of god, that of the lord of creatures, was brought low among the names of many gods and was nowhere to be found. And his offspring was led astray by them and was not serving him, for Hyle drew all to herself, and did not allow even a single one of them to serve him. Then, they say, the lord of creatures flew into a passion, because they left him and obeyed Hyle; and in his anger he began to cast into Gehenna one after another those who were leaving their bodies; and he cast Adam into Gehenna because of the tree; and so he cast all men into Gehenna for twenty-nine ages.

And, they say, when the good and stranger God, who was sitting in the third heaven, saw that so many generations were lost and tormented in between two betrayers, the lord of creatures and Hyle, he was grieved for those fallen into the fire and tormented. He sent his son to go and save them and to take the likeness of a slave and to be [fashioned] in the form of a man among the sons of the god of the law. " Heal," he said, " their lepers and raise their dead, open [the eyes of] their blind and work among them the very greatest healings freely; till the lord of creatures see thee and be envious and bring thee to a cross. And then at thy death thou shalt descend into hell and thou shalt bring them thence; for hell is not wont to receive life in its midst. And on that account thou dost ascend upon a cross, that thou mayest be like unto the dead and hell may open its mouth to receive thee and thou mayest enter into its midst and make it empty."

And when he had brought him to a cross, they say, he went down into hell and made it empty. And having brought the souls out of its midst, he led them to the third heaven to his father. And the lord of creatures, aroused to fury, in his anger tore his mantle and the veil of his temple and darkened his sun and clothed his world in black and sat grieving for sorrow.

Then Jesus descended the second time in the form of his deity to the lord of creatures and entered into judgment with him on account of his death. And when the lord of the world saw the deity of Jesus, he knew that there was another god besides himself. And Jesus said to him, " I have a law-suit with thee and let none judge between us, save the law, which thou didst write." And when they set the law in the midst, Jesus said to him: " Didst thou not write in thy law that he who shall kill, shall die, and that he who sheds the innocent man's blood, they shall shed his blood? " And he said, " Yes, I wrote it." And Jesus said to him: " Now give thyself into my hands, that I may kill thee and shed thy blood, as thou hast killed me and shed my blood, for I am truly juster than thou and I have done very great benefits to thy creatures." And [Jesus] began to recount the benefits that he had done to his creatures.

And when the lord of creatures saw that [Jesus] had overcome him and he did not know what to say, because by his own law was he condemned, and he found not how to give answer, for he was liable to [be put to] death in return for his death, then casting himself down in supplication, he begged him, [saying] ' Because I sinned and killed thee unwittingly, for I did not know that thou art a god, but I counted thee a man, it is granted thee in return for that offence to take all, who will believe in thee, where thou wilt.' Then Jesus, leaving him, took and seized Paul, and revealed to him the purchase price and sent him to preach that we are purchased with a purchase price, and that everyone, who believed in Jesus, has been sold by the just [god] to the good.

This is the beginning of the heresy of Marcion, apart from many other trivialities; and they do not all know this but a few of them do; and they hand on this teaching by [word of] mouth one to another; they say, the stranger has purchased us with a purchase price from the lord of creatures; but how and by what means we are purchased, that they do not all know.

C. S. C. WILLIAMS
Journal of Theological Studies 45 (1944), 65-73.
(*Reprinted by permission*)

4

Naassene Exegesis

In the fifth book of his ' Refutation of All Heresies,' Hippolytus gives
an account of the Naassenes which contains all that we know of them.
He has used at least two different documents in his account, and has
added his own confusion to that of the documents themselves. The date
of the Naassenes is difficult to determine, but the atmosphere of their
syncretistic hymns suggests a time not before the reign of Hadrian (117-
138), while one of their notions, that of the pre-existent Almond, may
have been parodied by Irenaeus (c. 180). On the date see A. D. Nock
in ' Journal of Hellenic Studies ' 49 (1929), 115.

The principal source of Hippolytus' information is a Naassene
commentary on a Phrygian hymn to Attis. For greater clarity we give
the hymn before selections from the commentary, reversing his order.

A. HYMN TO ATTIS

Whether thou art the offspring of Kronos or, blessed one, of
Zeus or of great Rhea—hail, Attis, at whose name Rhea looks
down. The Assyrians call thee thrice-lamented Adonis; all
Egypt, Osiris; Greek wisdom, the heavenly horn of the moon;
the Samothracians, venerable Adamnas; the Haemonians,
Corybant; and the Phrygians, sometimes Papas, sometimes
Corpse or God or Sterile or Goat-herd or Harvested Green
Sheaf, or Flute-player whom the Fertile Almond brought
forth.

HIPPOLYTUS, *Ref.* v. 9. 8.

B. THE NAASSENES

The Greeks say that Earth first brought forth Man, bearing a good gift and wishing to become the mother not of insensible plants or of irrational animals but of a tame animal loved by God. . . .

The Assyrians claim that among them was born Oannes, the fish-eater. The Chaldaeans make mention of Adam and say that this man was the only one whom the earth produced; he lay without breath and motionless and immovable, like a statue. He was an image of that man above, Adamas, and was made by many powers.

The great Man from above, from whom is derived " every family existing on earth and in the heavens " [Eph. 3: 15], had to be completely submissive, and therefore a soul was given him so that through the soul the " enslaved creature of the great and most excellent and perfect man " might suffer and be punished.

They also ask what the soul is and whence it originates and of what sort its nature is since it comes to man and by moving enslaves and punishes the " creature of the perfect man "; they inquire not from the Scriptures but from mystic doctrines.

HIPPOLYTUS, Ref. v. 7. 3-8.

He who says everything originated from one principle is wrong, but he who says it came from three is right and will give proof of the whole matter. For there is one blessed nature of the blessed Man above, Adamnas; one mortal nature below; and one kingless race which has ascended above, where there are Miriam the sought for and Jothor the great wise man and Zippora the seeing one and Moses, whose origin is not in Egypt because he had sons in Midian.

The poets also knew this.

" All things were divided in three and each received his lot of honour " [*Iliad* xv. 189]. The Magnitudes must be expressed, but expressed by everyone in every possible way so " that hearing they may not hear and seeing may not see " [Matt. 13: 13]. If the Magnitudes had not been expressed the universe could not have come into existence. These are the three supremely important words: Kaulakau, Saulasau, Zeesar [Is. 28: 10]: Kaulakau—the one above Adamas; Saulasau—the mortal below; Zeesar—the Jordan which flows upward.

This is the masculo-feminine Man who is in all, whom the ignorant call three-bodied Geryon as if his name meant " flowing from the earth " [*ge-ryon*]; the Greeks generally call him " the heavenly horn of the moon " [*menos-keras*] because he has mixed [*kata-me-miche*] and combined [*kekerake*] everything with everything else. " For all things came into existence through him, and apart from him Nothing came into existence. What came into existence in him is Life " [John 1: 3-4]. " Life " is the ineffable race of perfect men unknown to previous generations [cf. Eph. 3: 5]. " Nothing," which came into existence apart from him, is the world proper, which came into existence apart from him, made by the third and fourth gods.

HIPPOLYTUS, *Ref.* v. 8. 1-5.

C. THE EXEGESIS OF THE HYMN TO ATTIS

This is the great and ineffable mystery of the Samothracians which only the perfect—i.e., ourselves—are allowed to know. For in their mysteries the Samothracians have the explicit tradition that Adam is the archetypal man. In the temple of the Samothracians are erected two statues of naked men, with both hands, raised towards heaven and with their male members erect, like the statue of Hermes in Cyllene. These statues are images of the First Man and of the regenerated spiritual man who in every respect possesses the same nature as the First One.

This is what the Saviour meant when he said, " Unless

you drink my blood and eat my flesh, you will not enter the kingdom of heaven [John 6: 53]; but if you drink the cup which I drink [Mark 10: 38] you cannot enter where I go [John 8: 21]." For he knew the nature of each of his disciples, and he knew that each of them had to come to his proper nature. For he chose twelve disciples from the twelve tribes, and through them he spoke to every tribe; therefore not all hear the preachings of the twelve disciples, and if they do hear, they cannot accept them. For what is not according to nature is contrary to nature for them.

This Man is called *Corybant* by the Thracians who live by the Haemus river, and the Phrygians give him a similar name, because from the top of the head [*coryphe*] and from the unimprinted brain he begins his descent [*kata-ba-sis*] and passes through all the elements of the lower parts. We do not know how and in what way he comes down. This is the meaning of " we heard his voice but we did not see his appearance " [cf. John 5: 37]. For one hears his voice when he has been separated and imprinted, but no one knows what the form is which has come down from above, from the Unimprinted One. It is in the earthly creature, but no one knows it. This is the " God who dwells in the water-flood," according to the psalmbook, who makes utterance and cries out " from many waters " [Ps. 29: 10, 3]. The " many waters " is the manifold race of men, from among which he shouts and cries to the Unimprinted Man, saying, " Save my only daughter from the lions " [Ps. 22: 21-22]. To him was said, " You are my child, Israel; fear not; for if you go through rivers they will not engulf you, and if you go through fire it will not burn you " [Is. 41: 8, 43: 2]. " Rivers " is the moist matter of generation, " fire " the impulse and desire for generation; " you are mine, fear not." And again, " if a mother forgets to have compassion for her children or to give them the breast, I too will forget you " [Is. 49: 15]—Adamas says this to those who belong to him—" but if a woman forgets these things, I will not forget you; I have painted you on my hands " [Is. 49: 16].

And concerning his ascent, the regeneration by which he becomes spiritual and not carnal, the Scripture says: " Let your archons lift up the gates, and be lifted up, eternal gates, and the King of glory will enter " [Ps. 24: 7, 9]. This is the wonder of wonders, for " who is this King of glory? " [Ps. 24: 10]. " A worm and no man, the reproach of man and the one rejected by the people " [Ps. 22: 7]. " This is the King of glory, the one mighty in war " [Ps. 24: 10, 8]. " War " means the war in the body, for the creature was formed out of conflicting elements—as it is written, " Remember the war which takes place in the body " [Job. 40: 27]. Jacob saw this entrance and this gate when he went into Mesopotamia—i.e., passed from childhood to youth and manhood [" going into Mesopotamia "]. " Mesopotamia " is the course of the great Ocean, flowing from the midst of the Perfect Man. And he marvelled at the heavenly gate, saying, " How fearful is this place—it is no other than the house of God, and this is the gate of heaven " [Gen. 28: 17]. For this reason Jesus says, " I am the true gate " [John 10: 9]. He who speaks thus is the Perfect Man, imprinted from above from the Unimprinted One. The Perfect Man cannot be saved unless he is regenerated and enters through this gate.

The same Man is also called *Papas* by the Phrygians because he stopped [*e-pa-ysen*] everything [*panta*] which was in disorderly and confused motion before his appearance. The name Papas belongs to all the beings " in heaven, on earth, and under the earth " [Phil. 2: 10], when they say, " Stop, stop the discord of the universe and make ' peace for those afar,' i.e., material and earthly beings, and ' peace for those near ' [Eph. 2: 17], i.e., spiritual and intelligent men who are perfect."

The Phrygians also give him the name *Corpse*, because he is buried in the body as in a sepulchre and tomb. This is the meaning of " You are whitened tombs, full of dead men's bones within " [Matt. 23: 27]—for there is no living man among you—and again, " the dead will come forth from the sepulchres " [cf. John 5: 28; Matt. 27: 52-53]—i.e., from the earthly bodies, being regenerated as spiritual beings, not carnal. This is the resurrection which takes place through the gate of the heavens. All those who do not enter through it remain dead.

The Phrygians also call him *God* when he has been transformed. For he becomes God when he rises from the dead and through such a gate enters into heaven. The apostle Paul knew this gate: he half-opened it in a mystery and said that he had been " seized by an angel and taken to the second and third heaven, to Paradise itself, where he saw what he saw and heard ineffable words which a man is not allowed to relate " [2 Cor. 12: 2-4]. These are the ineffable mysteries of which all men speak, " which we speak in words taught not by human wisdom but by the Spirit, explaining spiritual matters to spiritual men. The psychic man does not accept what belongs to the Spirit of God, for to him it is foolishness " [1 Cor. 2: 13-14].

These are the ineffable mysteries of the Spirit, which we alone know. Of these the Saviour said, " No one can come to me unless my heavenly Father draws him " [John 6: 44]. For it is exceedingly difficult to receive and to take this great and ineffable mystery. And again, the Saviour said, " Not everyone who says to me, Lord, Lord, will enter into the kingdom of heaven, but he who does the will of my Father in heaven " [Matt. 7: 21]. And to show that doers, not hearers only [cf. James 1:22], must enter the kingdom of heaven, he said again, " The tax-collectors and prostitutes precede you into the kingdom of heaven " [Matt. 21: 31]. " Tax-collectors " are those who receive duties [*tele*] on everything and we are the tax-collectors " to whom the taxes [*tele*] of the aeons have come " [1 Cor. 10: 11]. The " taxes " [or perfections] are the seeds sown in the universe by the Unimprinted One; through them the whole universe is completed [*syn-teleitai*], for through them it began to come into existence. This is the meaning of the saying: " The sower went forth to sow, and some fell by the way and were trodden down; others fell on rocky ground and sprang up and, because they had no depth, withered and died;

and others fell on beautiful and good ground and produced fruit—one a hundred, another sixty, another thirty. He who has ears to hear, let him hear " [Matt. 13: 3-9]. This means that no one has been a hearer of these mysteries except the perfect gnostics alone. This is the " beautiful and good " which Moses mentions: " I will lead you into a beautiful and good land, into a land flowing with milk and honey." [Deut. 31: 20]. " Honey and milk " are what the perfect taste in order to become kingless and to share in the Pleroma. The Pleroma is that through which all created beings come into existence and are completed from the uncreated.

The Phrygians also give him the name *Sterile*. He is sterile when he is fleshly and performs the " lust of the flesh " [Gal. 5: 16]. This is what is meant by " every tree which does not bring forth good fruit is cut down and cast into fire " [Matt. 3: 10]. The " fruits " are only the rational, the living men, who enter through the third gate. The Naassenes say, " If you ate dead things and made them living, what will you do if you eat living things? " [*Gospel of Thomas, 10*] What they call " living " are rational principles and intelligences and men, pearls which the Unimprinted One has cast as fruits into the creation. This is the meaning of " do not cast what is holy to the dogs, nor pearls to swine " [Matt. 7: 6]. The work of swine and dogs is the intercourse of woman with man.

The Phrygians also call him *Goatherd* [*Aipolos*], not because he feeds goats, as the psychic men call them, but because he is ever-turning [*aei-polos*], i.e., always turning and circulating and impressing the whole universe with turning motion. For to turn [*polein*] is to circulate and alter matters; for this reason the two centres of the heaven are called poles. And the poet also said:

An old man, wave-dwelling, frequently comes [*poleitai*] here—
immortal Proteus, the Egyptian [*Odyss.* iv. 384-85].

Poleitai does not mean that he is sold but that he turns about and goes around. Furthermore, cities [*poleis*] in which we live are so-called because we turn and circulate in them. Thus the Phrygians call *Aipolos* the one who always turns things in every direction and transfers them to his own domain.

The Phrygians also call him *Fertile*, because " the children of the deserted woman are more than those of the one who has a husband " [Is. 54: 1, Gal. 4: 27], i.e., those who are reborn immortal and endure for ever are immortal, even though few of them are born; all carnal beings are perishable, even though very many of them are born. That is why " Rachel wept for her children and did not want to be comforted for them; for she knew that they were not " [Jer. 31: 15; Matt. 2: 18]. Jeremiah too mourns for the Jerusalem below, not the city in Phoenicia but the perishable generation below; for Jeremiah knew the Perfect Man, who is regenerated " from water and spirit " [John 3: 5], not the carnal one. It was Jeremiah who said, " He is Man, and who will know him? " [Jer. 17: 9]—this shows how deep and difficult to comprehend is the knowledge [*gnosis*] of the Perfect Man. For the knowledge of Man is the beginning of perfection, while the finished perfection is the knowledge of God.

The Phrygians also call him the *Harvested Green Sheaf*. According to them the Athenians give him the same name when they hold Eleusinian initiations and silently show the inititiates the great and marvellous and most perfect of the mysteries there, the harvested sheaf. For the Athenians, this sheaf is the great and perfect torch which comes from the Unimprinted One. This is what the hierophant declares; he is not castrated like Attis, but is made a eunuch by means of hemlock and has given up all carnal generation. By night in Eleusis with great light he performs the great and and ineffable mysteries and cries out, " Brimo has borne a holy child, Brimos "—i.e., the strong woman has borne a strong child. " Holy " is the generation which is spiritual, heavenly, above; " strong " is the one thus born. This mystery is called Eleusis and sanctuary of Demeter [*anactoreion*]: " Eleusis," because we spirituals have come from above, flowing down from

Adamnas [*eleusesthai* means "to come"]; *anactoreion*, from
"ascending above" [*anelthein ano*]. This is what the Eleusinian
initiates call the great mysteries; it is a law that those who
are initiated into the lesser mysteries should later be initiated
into the great ones. For greater lots acquire greater parts
[Heraclitus, fr. 25 Diels]. The lesser mysteries are those of the
Persephone below. Concerning these mysteries and the way
which leads there—"broad and spacious" [Matt. 7: 13] and
bearing to Persephone those who are destroyed—the poet also
said:

> "Beneath her is a horrible pathway, hollow and
> muddy;
> it is excellent to lead to the lovely grove of Aphrodite
> the much-honoured."

These are the lesser mysteries of carnal generation. After
initiation into them men ought to terminate the lesser and be
initiated into the great and heavenly ones. For those who
acquire lots connected with the latter will receive greater parts.

This is the gate of heaven and the house of God, where the
good God dwells alone, where no impure man enters, no
psychic, no carnal. It is reserved for the spirituals alone, and
those who come there must put on the wedding garments and
all become bridegrooms, made more masculine by the virginal
spirit. This is the virgin who is pregnant and conceives and
bears a son [Is. 7: 14]—a son who is not psychic or corporeal
but is the blessed Aeon of Aeons. Concerning these matters
the Saviour expressly said, "Narrow and straitened is the way
which leads to life, and there are few who enter it; but broad
and spacious is the way which leads to destruction, and there
are many who enter through it" [Matt. 7: 13-14].

The Phrygians also say that the Father of All is an *Almond*
[*amygdalos*]—not the tree, but that pre-existent almond which
has within itself the perfect fruit, palpitating [so to speak] and
moving in the interior; it rent its own womb and brought
forth its invisible and unnameable and ineffable child, of
which we are speaking. To rend [*amyxia*] is to tear and cut

through, just as physicians call " scarifications " [*amychas*] the incisions which they make in inflamed bodies or in those which contain some tumour. Thus the Phrygians give the name " almond " to the being from which the invisible one came forth and was begotten, " through whom everything came into existence and apart from him the non-existent was made " [John 1: 3].

The being thus born is called *Flute-player*, because what was born is a harmonious breath [or spirit]. For " God is a Spirit; therefore the true worshippers will worship neither on this mountain nor in Jerusalem, but in spirit " [John 4: 21, 23-24]. For the worship of the perfect ones is spiritual, not carnal. The Spirit is there where the Father and the Son are named, the Son born there of the Father. He is the many-named one, many-eyed, incomprehensible, towards which every nature strives, each in its own way. He is the expressed Word [*rhema*] of God, which is the Word of Declaration of the Great Power; therefore it is sealed and hidden and veiled, lying in the dwelling, on which the root of All is founded— the root of aeons, powers, thoughts, gods, angels, envoy spirits, existent and non-existent, generated and ungenerated, incomprehensible and comprehensible, years, months, days, hours, and an indivisible point from which the smallest being will come forth to grow, part by part; the non-existent un-derived indivisible point will, by its own thought, become some incomprehensible greatness. This is the kingdom of heaven, the grain of mustard seed, the indivisible point existing in the body, which no one knows except the spirituals alone. This is the meaning of " there are no words or language, whose voices are not heard " [Ps. 19: 3].

HIPPOLYTUS, *Ref.* v. 8. 9—9. 6.

On the Naassenes see R. P. Casey, " Naassenes and Ophites," ' Journal of Theological Studies ' 27 (1925-26), 374-87; A. D. Nock in ' Journal of Hellenic Studies.'

D. NAASSENE HYMN

The generative law of the universe was first-born Mind;
The second principle after the first-born was confused chaos;
The third rank in the working of this law fell to the soul [(?)
    the text is corrupt].

Therefore, clothed in a watery form, she grieves, toy and slave
    of death.
Sometimes, invested with royalty, she sees light:
Sometimes, fallen into evil, she weeps.
    Sometimes she weeps and sometimes she rejoices;
    Sometimes she weeps and sometimes she is judged;
    Sometimes she is judged and sometimes she dies.
Sometimes she finally finds no exit, because her wandering ways
    have led to a labyrinth of evils.

Then Jesus said: Look, Father! A prey to evils, she wanders
    still on earth, far from your breath; she tries to flee
    from the odious chaos and does not know how to
    pass through it.
    Therefore send me, Father; I will descend, bearing the
      seals.
    I will pass through all aeons;
    I will reveal all mysteries;
    I will show the forms of gods;
And I will deliver, under the name of *gnosis*, the secrets of the
    holy way.

HIPPOLYTUS, *Ref.* v. 10. 2

5

The Hymn of the Pearl

This hymn, often called the hymn or song of the pearl, is preserved in two versions of the apocryphal ' Acts of Thomas,' which date from the third century; it reflects late Valentinian doctrine, perhaps that of Bardaisan (A.D. 154-222). The " filthy and unclean garb " of the soul is the body (verse 62); the " King of kings " is evidently the Father, while the " Queen of the East " is the Mother, and the " next in rank " is the Son of the Living.

One version of the ' Acts of Thomas,' in Syriac, preserves the metrical form of the hymn, which has been translated by A. A. Bevan in 'Texts and Studies' (Cambridge, 1897) V, 3; this translation is reprinted here as revised by W. R. Schoedel. The Greek version is to be found in R. A. Lipsius—M. Bonnet, ' Acta Apostolorum Apocrypha ' II, 2 (Leipzig, 1903), 218-24.

On the hymn see H. H. Schaeder, " Bardesanes von Edessa," ' Zeitschrift für Kirchengeschichte ' 51 (1932), 21-73; H. Jonas, ' Gnosis und spätantiker Geist ' I (Gottingen, 1934), 320-28; G. Widengren, " Der iranische Hintergrund der Gnosis," "Zeitschrift für Religions- und Geistesgeschichte ' 4 (1952), 97-114; A. Adam, ' Beihefte zür Zeitschrift fur die neutestamentlicke Wissenschaft ' 24 (Berlin, 1959), 48-75.

(108) 1 When I was a little child,
         And dwelling in my kingdom in my Father's house,
      2 And in the wealth and the glories
         Of my nurturers had my pleasure,

3 From the East, our home,
My parents, having equipped me, sent me forth.

4 And of the wealth of our treasury
They had already tied up for me a load,

5 Large it was, yet light,
So that I might bear it unaided—

6 Gold from the land of Ellaie
And silver of Gazzak the great,

7 And rubies of India,
And agates [?] from the land of Kushan [?]

8 And they girded me with adamant
Which can crush iron.

9 And they took off from me the bright robe,
Which in their love they had wrought for me,

10 And my purple toga,
Which was measured [and] woven to my stature.

11 And they made a compact with me,
And wrote it in my heart that it should not be forgotten:

12 " If thou goest down into Egypt,
And bringest the one pearl,

13 Which is in the midst of the sea
Hard by the loud-breathing serpent,

14 [Then] shalt thou put on thy bright robe
And thy toga, which is laid over it,

15 And with thy Brother, our next in rank,
Thou shalt be heir in our kingdom."

(109) 16 I quitted the East [and] went down,
There being with me two messengers,

17 For the way was dangerous and difficult,
And I was very young to tread it.

18 I passed the borders of Maishan,
The meeting-place of the merchants of the East,

19 And I reached the land of Babel
And entered the walls of Sarbug;

20 I went down into Egypt,
And my companions parted from me.

21 I betook me straight to the serpent,
   Hard by his dwelling I abode,

22 [Waiting] till he should slumber and sleep,
   And I could take my pearl from him.

23 And when I was single and alone,
   A stranger to those with whom I dwelt,

24 One of my race, a free-born man,
   From among the Easterns, I beheld there—

25 A youth fair and well favoured,
   [a son of great rulers.]

26
   . . . and he came and attached himself to me.

27 And I made him my intimate,
   A comrade with whom I shared my merchandise.

28 I warned him against the Egyptians
   And against consorting with the unclean;

29 And I put on a garb like theirs,
   Lest they should recognise me because I had come
   from afar.

30 To take away the pearl,
   And [lest] they should arouse the serpent against me.

31 But in some way or other
   They perceived that I was not their countryman;

32 So they dealt with me treacherousl ,
   Moreover they gave me their food to eat

33 I forgot that I was a son of kings,
   And I served their king;

34 And I forgot the pearl,
   For which my parents had sent me,

35 And by reason of the burden of their foods
   I lay in a deep sleep.

(110) 36 But all these things that befell me
   My parents perceived and were grieved for me;

37 And a proclamation was made in our kingdom,
   That all should speed to our gate,

38 Kings and princes of Parthia
   And all the nobles of the East.

39 So they wove a plan on my behalf,
   That I might not be left in Egypt,

40 And they wrote to me a letter,
   And every noble signed his name thereto:

41 " From thy Father, the King of kings,
   And thy Mother, the mistress of the East,

42 And from thy Brother, our next in rank,
   To thee our son, who art in Egypt, greeting!

43 Up and arise from thy sleep,
   And listen to the words of our letter!

44 Call to mind that thou art a son of kings!
   See the slavery—whom thou servest!

45 Remember the pearl
   For which thou didst speed to Egypt!

46 Think of thy bright robe,
   And remember thy glorious toga,

47 Which thou shalt put on as thine adornment,
   When thy name hath been read out in the book of
   the valiant,

48 And with thy Brother, our deputy,
   Thou shalt be a dweller in our kingdom."

(111) 49 And my letter [was] a letter
   Which the King sealed with his right hand,

50 [To keep it] from the wicked ones, the children of
   Babel,
   And from the savage demons of Sarbug.

51 It flew in the likeness of an eagle,
   The king of all birds ;

52 It flew and alighted beside me,
   And became all speech.

53 At its voice and the sound of its rustling,
   I started and arose from my sleep.

54 I took it up and kissed it,
   And loosed its seal [?], [and] read:

55 And according to what was traced on my heart.
   Were the words of my letter written.

56 I remembered that I was a son of kings,

And my freedom longed for its own nature.

57 I remembered the pearl,
For which I had been sent to Egypt,

58 And I began to charm him,
The terrible loud-breathing serpent.

59 I hushed him to sleep and lulled him into slumber,
For my Father's name I named over him,

60 And the name of our next in rank,
And of my Mother, the queen of the East;

61 And I snatched away the pearl,
And turned to go back to my Father's house.

62 And their filthy and unclean garb
I stripped off, and left it in their country,

63 And I took my way straight to come
To the light of our home, the East.

64 And my letter, my awakener,
I found before me on the road,

65 And as with its voice it had awakened me
[So] too with its light it was leading me

66 For the royal garment of silk
Shone before me with its form,

67 And with its voice and its guidance
It also encouraged me to speed,

68 And with its love was drawing me on.

69 I went forth, passed by Sarbug.
I left Babel on my left hand,

70 And reached Maishan the great,
The haven of the merchants,

71 That sitteth on the shore of the sea.

72 And my bright robe, which I had stripped off,
And the toga where it was wrapped,

73 From the heights of Hyrcania [?]
My parents sent thither,

74 By the hand of their treasurers,
Who in their faithfulness could be trusted therewith.

(112) 75 And because I remembered not its fashion—

For in my childhood I had left it in my Father's
house—

76 On a sudden, as I faced it,
The garment seemed to me like a mirror of myself.

77 I saw it all in my whole self,
Moreover I faced my whole self in [facing] it,

78 For we were two in distinction
And yet again one in one likeness.

79 And the treasurers also,
Who brought it to me, I saw in like manner,

80 That they were twain [yet] one likeness,
For there was graven on them one sign of the
King,

81 Whose hands [they were] which restored to me[?]
My treasure and my wealth by means of them,

82 My bright embroidered robe,
which was decorated with glorious colours;

83 With gold and with beryls,
And rubies and agates [?]

84 And sardonyxes varied in colour,
It also was made ready in its home on high,

85 And with stones of adamant
All its seams were fastened;

86 And the image of the King of kings
Was depicted in full all over it,

87 And like the sapphire-stone also
Were its manifold hues.

(113) 88 And again I saw that all over it
The motions of knowledge were stirring,

89 And as if to speak
I saw it also making itself ready.

90 I heard the sound of its tones,
Which it uttered to those who brought it down [?]

91 Saying, " I am he who is mighty in deeds
I whom they reared for him in the presence of my
father,

92 And I also perceived in myself

That my stature was growing according to his labours."

93 And in its kingly motions
It was spreading itself out towards me,

94 And in the hands of its givers
It hastened that I might take it.

95 And me too my love urged on
That I should run to meet it and receive it,

96 And I stretched forth and received it,
With the beauty of its colours I adorned myself.

97 And my toga of brilliant colours
I cast around me, in its whole breadth.

98 I clothed myself therewith, and ascended
To the gate of salutation and homage;

99 I bowed my head, and did homage
To the Majesty of my Father who had sent it to me,

100 For I had done his commandments,
And he too had done what he promised,

101 And at the gate of his princes,
I mingled with his nobles;

102 For he rejoiced in me and received me,
And I was with him in his kingdom.

103 And with the voice of praise
All his servants glorify him.

104 And he promised that also to the gate
Of the King of kings I should speed with him,

105 And bringing my gift and my pearl
I should appear with him before our King.

A. A. BEVAN, *Texts and Studies* V, pp. 10-31.
(*Revised and corrected by* W. R. SCHOEDEL).

PART IV

BASILIDES AND ISIDORE

We have already found an account of Basilidian doctrine in Irenaeus, ' Adv. haer.' i. 24. 3-7 (Part I, 4). A description which is almost completely different is provided by Hippolytus, ' Refutatio' vii. 20-27, and in the view of most scholars this is the genuine system of Basilides (see P. Hendrix, ' De Alexandrijnsche Haeresiarch Basilides,' Amsterdam, 1926; J. H. Waszink, " Basilides," ' Reallexikon für Antike und Christentum' I, 1217-25.)

In addition to Hippolytus' description, we possess several fragments from Basilides' writings. The second, from the fourth-century ' Acta Archelai,' contains a report not of Basilides' own thoughts but of the views of " barbarians," though presumably he found these views attractive. Other fragments, including those from Basilides' son Isidore, reflect Basilidian concern with ancient tradition and with ethical problems.

In spite of the semi-philosophical dress of much of this teaching, its foundation lies not in philosophy but in Gnostic revelation and experience, as Quispel has shown (G. Quispel, " L'homme gnostique," ' Eranos-Jahrbücher' 16, 1948, 89-139).

I

Basilides' System

(20, 2) There was a time when there was nothing, but " nothing " was not anything existent. Simply and plainly, without any sophistry, there was absolutely nothing. When I say " was," I do not mean that anything " was," but I say it in order to signify what I want to show—I mean that there was absolutely nothing. (3) What is called by a name is not absolutely ineffable; we may call it ineffable, but it is not ineffable, for the [truly] ineffable is not ineffable but " above every name which is named " [Eph. 1: 21]. (4) Names are not sufficient for designating all the objects in the world, because they are innumerable; names are inadequate. I do not undertake to find proper names for all. Instead, by understanding without speech one must receive the properties of the things named. Homonyms have produced trouble and error for those who hear.

(21, 1) Since, then, there was nothing—no matter, no substance, no non-substance, nothing simple, nothing complex, nothing not understood, nothing not sensed, no man, no angel, no god, not anything that is named or perceived through sense, not any intelligible things, and not anything which can be defined more subtly than anything else—the non-existent God wished, without intelligence, without sense, without will, without choice, without passion, without desire, to make a universe [*cosmos*]. (2) I say that he " wished " for the sake of saying something, but it was [actually] without wish, without intelligence, without sense; and I say " universe " in reference not to the one with breadth and divisibility which came into existence later and continued to exist, but to the seed of the universe. (3) The seed of the universe had everything within it, just as the grain of mustard seed [Matt. 13: 31-32], collecting everything in the smallest space, contains it all together— roots, stem, branches, innumerable leaves, seeds of the grains generated from the plant, and seeds of still other plants, when they are scattered.

(4) Thus the non-existent God made a non-existent universe out of the non-existent, establishing and giving substance to one certain seed which had within it the whole semination of the universe. (5) It is like the egg of some variegated and many-coloured bird, such as the peacock or some other bird which is even more multiform and many-coloured, an egg which though one has within it many forms of multiform, many-coloured, many-constituted substances. Thus the non-existent seed, established by the non-existent God as the semination of the universe, was at the same time polymorphous and many-substanced.

(22, 1) Everything, then, of which one can speak, and even of which one cannot speak because it does not exist; everything which was necessarily going to adapt itself to the universe which was to come from the seed and at proper times be given growth by such a God, so great that the creation cannot speak of him or contain him in thought;—all these beings existed, deposited in the seed, just as we see in the case of the newborn child; we see the teeth which grow later, the paternal substance, intelligence, and all the things man does not have at first but gradually acquires as he grows up.

(2) Why do we need " emanation " or why do we posit " matter " in order for God to make the universe, as if he were a spider making a web or a mortal man using bronze or wood or pieces of material? (3) " He spoke and it was done " [Ps. 33: 9]; this is what the expression of Moses means: " Let there be light; and there was light " [Gen. 1: 3]. Whence came the light? From nothing; for we are told not what its source was but only that it came from the voice which spoke.

He who speaks did not exist, nor did what came into existence.
(4) For the seed of the universe came into existence out of
the non-existent, i.e., the word which was spoken: "Let
there be light." And this is what the gospels mean when they
say, "It was true light, which illuminates every man coming
into the universe" [John 1: 9]. (5) Man originates from that
seed and is illuminated from it.

(6) Do not ask about the origin of what I say came into
existence after this. For the seed of the universe had all the
seeds deposited and contained within itself, just as, though non-
existent, they were planned for by the non-existent God.
(7) In this seed there was a Triple Sonship, in every respect
having the same nature [*homoousios*] as that of the non-existent
God; it was generated out of the non-existent. Of this Triple
Sonship one part was subtle, another opaque, and the third
in need of purification.

(8) At the moment when the seed was first cast forth by
the non-existent God, the subtle part pulsated and ascended
and ran upwards from below, as the poet says, "like a wing
or like thought" [*Odyss.* vii. 36], and came to the Non-existent.
For every being, each in its own way, is drawn by the extra-
ordinary beauty and loveliness of him. (9) The more opaque
part, remaining in the seed, wanted to imitate the first, but
could not run upwards because it was much less subtle than
the Sonship which ran upwards by itself. So it was left behind.
(10) Then this more opaque Sonship winged itself with the
Holy Spirit, which the Sonship puts on and benefits and from
which it receives benefit. (11) It benefits the Spirit, because
a bird's wing, separated from the bird, could never by itself fly
upwards on high; it is benefited, because a bird which has
lost a wing could never fly upwards on high. This is the
relation of the Sonship to the Holy Spirit and that of the
Holy Spirit to the Sonship. (12) The Sonship, borne upwards
by the Spirit as by a wing, bears up the wing [i.e. the Spirit].
Coming close to the subtle Sonship and the non-existent God
who created out of the non-existent, it was not able to keep
the Spirit with itself; for the Spirit was not of the same sub-

stance or nature as the Sonship. (13) As pure and dry air is unnatural and deadly for fish, so it was contrary to nature for the Holy Spirit to remain in that place more ineffable that what is ineffable and " above all names," the place of the non-existent God and the Sonship. Then the Sonship left the Spirit near that blessed place, which cannot be conceived of or expressed in any word. It was not entirely deserted or abandoned by the Sonship; (14) but as when a most odoriferous perfume is once put in a vase, one can most carefully empty the vase, but a certain odour of perfume still remains even if the vessel is emptied, and the vessel retains the odour if not the perfume—so the Holy Spirit, separated from the Sonship and deprived of it, still keeps the power of the perfume, the odour of the Sonship. (15) This is what the psalmist means by saying, " Like perfume on Aaron's head which came down on his beard " [Ps. 133: 2]. He means the perfume borne from above from the Holy Spirit down to the formless and distant place where we are, from which the Sonship began his ascent, borne as on the wings and back of an eagle [cf. Deut. 32: 11]. (16) All beings desire to rise above from below, from the worse to the better; nothing is so unintelligent as to descend from the better.

The third Sonship, which needed purification, remained in the great Heap of the mixture of seeds, giving and receiving benefit. (23, 1) And after the first and second ascent of the Sonship(s), the Holy Spirit remained as described, set as a " firmament " [Gen. 1: 6] between supermundane being and the universe. (2) Existent beings are divided into two classes and categories: the first is called " universe " [*cosmos*], the second " supermundane " [*hypercosmical*]; the dividing line between the universe and the supermundane is the Spirit, which is holy and has the odour of the Sonship remaining in it. (3) When the firmament above the heaven had come into existence, then from the cosmic Seed and the Heap of the mixture of seeds there pulsated and was begotten the great Archon, the Head of the universe, whose beauty and size and power cannot be expressed. For he is more ineffable than what is ineffable and more powerful than what is powerful and wiser than the wise and greater than any good things you might possibly mention. (4) After being begotten, he raised himself and went upwards and the whole of him was borne above to the firmament, where he stood, regarding the firmament as the end of his ascent and exaltation and not imagining that there was anything at all beyond these things. He then became, of all the elements of the universe which were below, the wisest, the most powerful, the most excellent, the most luminous—in short, he surpassed everything remarkably good which you might possibly mention, save only the Sonship which still remained in the mixture of seeds; for he did not know that this Sonship was wiser, more powerful, and better than he. (5) Regarding himself as Lord and Master and Wise Builder [cf. 1 Cor. 3: 10], he turned to the creation of various parts of the universe. First he decided not to remain alone, and from the materials below he made for himself and begot a son much better and wiser than himself. (6) [All these things had been planned in advance by the non-existent God when he established the mixture of seeds]. When he saw his son, he marvelled and loved him and was amazed—so great did the beauty of the son of the great Archon appear to him —and the Archon seated him at his right hand. (7) This is the Eight where the great Archon is seated. For the great wise Demiurge made the whole heavenly creation; his son worked in him and advised him, since he was much wiser than the Demiurge.

(24, 3) When all [these] things had been fashioned, another Archon arose from the mixture of seeds; he was greater than everything below him except the Sonship which had been left below, but he was much inferior to the first Archon. This Archon too is called ineffable. (4) His place is called the Seven, and he is the governor and fashioner of everything below. He too made a son for himself out of the mixture of seeds, and as in the case of the first Archon, the son was more intelligent and wiser than the father. (5) In this space is the Heap and mixture of seeds, and the beings born there are born naturally. They hasten to be brought forth by the one [the non-existent God] who tells what is to happen—when, what, and how it must occur. They have no governor or caretaker or Demiurge; what suffices for them is the thought which the Non-existent thought when he made them.

(25, 1) When the whole universe and the supermundane were finished and lacked nothing more, there still remained in the mixture of seeds the third Sonship, which had been left in the seed to give and receive benefit. It was necessary for the abandoned Sonship to be revealed and to be restored above, above the dividing Spirit, to the subtle Sonship and to the one which imitated it and to the Non-existent: as it is written, " The creation itself groans and suffers pangs, awaiting the revelation of the sons of God " [Rom. 8: 19, 22] (2) [We spiritual beings are sons, left down here to adorn and fashion and correct and perfect the souls below which have a nature such as to remain in this space.] " From Adam to Moses sin reigned," as it is written [Rom. 5: 13-14]; (3) for the great Archon, who extends to the firmament, was reigning, thinking that he alone was God and that above him was nothing [Deut. 32: 39; Is. 45: 5]; for everything was kept in secret silence. This is the " mystery which was not revealed to former generations " [Col. 1: 26]. In those times the great Archon, the Eight, seemed to be King and Lord of all. (4) The Seven was King and Lord of this space [below], and while the Eight is ineffable, the Seven can be named. It was this Archon of the Seven who spoke to Moses and said, " I am the God of Abraham and Isaac and Jacob, and I did not reveal the name of God to them " [Exod. 6: 2-3]*—the name of the ineffable Archon-god of the Eight. (5) All the prophets before the Saviour spoke from this source [cf. John 10: 8].

When it was necessary for us to be revealed as the children of God [concerning whom " the creation groaned and was in pangs, awaiting the revelation "], the Gospel came into the

---

* As Hippolytus notes, the text reads " I am the Lord; and I appeared to Abraham and Isaac and Jacob, being their God, and I did not reveal my name ' Lord ' to them."

universe and passed through every principality and power and dominion and every name that is named [cf. Eph. 1:21]. (6) It really came, even though nothing came down from above and though the blessed Sonship did not depart from that inconceivable and blessed non-existent God. Just as Indian naphtha kindles fire even from a great distance, simply by appearing, so the powers reached upwards from the shapeless mass to the Sonship above. (7) For like Indian naphtha, the Gospel kindles and seizes thoughts, just as even the son of the great Archon of the Eight is kindled from the blessed Sonship beyond the dividing line. For the power of the Sonship in the midst of the Holy Spirit in the dividing line transmitted the fluid and attracted thoughts of the Sonship to the son of the great Archon. (26, 1) Then the Gospel first came from the Sonship, through the son seated by the Archon, to the Archon. The Archon learned that he was not the God of all but had been begotten, and that he had his own treasure laid up, above the ineffable and unnameable Non-existent and the Sonship. He was converted and was afraid, recognising his previous state of ignorance. (2) This is what is meant by, "The beginning of wisdom is the Lord's fear" [Ps. 111:10]. For he began to become wise, instructed by the Christ [son] who sat by him. He learned who the Non-existent is, who the Sonship is, what the Holy Spirit is, what the constitution of the universe is, and how the restoration will take place. (3) This is the "wisdom spoken in a mystery" [1 Cor. 2:7], concerning which the Scripture says, "Not in words taught by human wisdom, but in those taught by the Spirit" [1 Cor. 2:13]. After being instructed, taught, and made to fear, the Archon made a confession of the sin which he had committed by magnifying himself. (4) This is what is meant by, "I recognised my sin and I know my iniquity, which I will confess to the Aeon" [Ps. 32:5, 51:5]. When the great Archon had been instructed, the whole creation of the Eight was instructed and taught and the mystery was made known to the heavenly beings [cf. Eph. 3:9-10].

The Gospel still had to come to the Seven so that the

Archon of the Seven might similarly be taught and evangelised. (5) The son of the great Archon shone on the son of the Archon of the Seven with the light which he himself had, having kindled it from the Sonship. The son of the Archon of the Seven was illuminated and preached the Gospel to the Archon of the Seven and, as in the first case, this Archon was made to fear and made his confession. (6) When everything in the Seven had been illuminated and the Gospel had been proclaimed among them—for in the spaces themselves there exist innumerable creatures and principalities and powers and authorities; then 365 heavens, whose great Archon is Abrasax because his name contains the number 365; the number which this name represents contains everything and therefore the year consists of this number of days [cf. Irenaeus, *Adv. haer.* i. 24].—(7) it was still necessary to illuminate the formless space where we live, and to reveal the " mystery not known to former generations " to the Sonship which like an abortion had been abandoned in the formless space [cf. 1 Cor. 15: 8; Gal. 1: 16]—as it is written, " By revelation the mystery was made known to me " [Eph. 3: 3] and " I heard ineffable words which it is not lawful for a man to utter " [2 Cor. 12: 4].

(8) Then the light came down from the Seven [it had come down from the Eight above to the son of the Seven] upon Jesus the son of Mary, and he was illuminated and set on fire by the light which shone upon him. (9) This is what is meant by, " Holy Spirit will come upon you " [Luke 1: 35]; it had come from the Sonship through the dividing Spirit upon the Eight and the Seven and as far as Mary. And " Power of the Most High will overshadow you ": the power of judgment from the height above, through the Demiurge, down to the creation; this power belongs to the son.

(10) The universe remains in this condition until the whole Sonship left below to benefit the souls, in their shapeless state, and to receive benefit by being refashioned, follows Jesus and ascends above and comes there after being purified. It becomes very tenuous so that it can ascend of its own accord as the first Sonship ascended. For it holds the whole power

physically consolidated with it through the light which from above shone downward.

(27, 1) When the whole Sonship comes to be above the dividing line [the Spirit], then the creation will obtain mercy. To the present day it " groans and is tormented and awaits the revelation of the sons of God," in order that all the men of the Sonship may return thence. When this takes place, God will bring the great Ignorance upon the whole universe so that everything may remain in accordance with nature and nothing may desire anything contrary to nature. (2) All the souls of this space which have a nature such as to remain immortal only in this space will remain; they will know nothing different from this space or better than it. There will be no report or knowledge [*gnosis*] of things above in things below, so that the souls below will not be tormented by the desire of what is impossible, like a fish desiring to graze on the mountains with sheep; for such a desire would mean destruction for them. (3) Everything which remains in its place is imperishable; it is perishable only if it wants to pass beyond its natural limits. Thus the Archon of the Seven will know nothing of things above; the great Ignorance will overcome even him, so that " grief and pangs and groaning " [Is. 35: 10, 51: 11] will depart from him; for he will desire nothing impossible and will not be grieved. (4) Similarly the same ignorance will overcome even the great Archon of the Eight and [to an equal extent] all the creatures lying below him, so that he will not desire anything contrary to nature or suffer grief.

Thus the restoration of all things will take place. In the beginning they were established in accordance with nature in the seed of the universe. At the proper seasons they will be restored [cf. 1 Tim. 6: 15]. (5) Each has its own proper season; this is proved by the Saviour's saying, " My hour has not yet come " [John 2: 4], as well as by the magi who saw the star [Matt. 2: 1-2]. For the Saviour himself was subject to the influence of the stars and had planned in advance, in the great Mass, the hour of restoration.

(6) This is the " inner man " [Rom. 7: 22, Eph. 3: 16],

the spiritual in the psychic. It is the Sonship leaving the soul there, not because it was mortal but because it remained there in accordance with its own nature, just as the first Sonship left the Holy Spirit, the dividing line, in its proper place above and then put on its own soul.

(7) The Gospel is that knowledge [*gnosis*] of the super-mundane things which the great Archon did not know. When it was made known to him that there is the Holy Spirit [the dividing line], and the Sonship, and the non-existent God, the cause of all these, he rejoiced and was glad because of what was said.

(8) After Jesus came into existence in the way we have described, everything took place as it is written in the gospels. These things happened so that Jesus might become the first-fruits of the differentiation among confused beings. (9) Since the universe is divided into an Eight [the head of the whole universe; the great Archon is the head of the whole universe] and into a Seven [the Demiurge of things below is the head of the Seven] and into this space where we live [where formless-ness is], it was necessary for the confused beings to be differentiated through the differentiation which Jesus effected. (10) The bodily part of his being suffered; since it came from formlessness it was restored to formlessness. The psychic part of his being rose again, since it belonged to the Seven, and was restored to the Seven. He raised the part which belonged to the height of the great Archon, and it remained with the great Archon. He bore above the part which belonged to the dividing Spirit, and it remained in the dividing Spirit. (11) The Third Sonship was purified through him [the one abandoned to give and receive benefit], and it ascended to the blessed Sonship after passing through all these levels. (12) Jesus, then, became the first-fruits of the differentiation, and his suffering took place only for the differentiation of what was confused. In this way the whole Sonship left behind in the formless space in order to give and receive benefit must be differentiated as Jesus himself was differentiated.

HIPPOLYTUS, *Ref.* vii. 20-27.

2

Fragments

(1) For us, as we write the thirteenth book of treatises, the saving Word will provide the necessary and fertile word; through the parable of the Rich and Poor [Luke 16: 19-31] it shows us a nature without Root and without Place returning above to the things from which it had originated.

(2) [about 50 verses later] Let us cease from vain and inquisitive variety, and inquire more concerning the investigations of the barbarians in regard to good and evil and the opinions they have reached concerning them. For some of them say that there are two first principles of all things; they associate good and evil with them and say that they are the uncreated eternal beginnings. In the beginning there were Light and Darkness, existing self-sufficiently, not the ones said to have been created. Since these existed of themselves, each one properly led the life it wished and chose for itself. What is proper and does not seem evil to oneself is pleasing to all. But after each of them arrived at knowledge of the other and the Darkness contemplated the Light, overcome as with the desire for a better thing it attacked it and desired to share in it. Although the Darkness did these things, the Light accepted nothing at all of the Darkness into itself, nor did it come to desire the Darkness, except that it experienced the desire [*libido*] of looking at it; and it did look at the Darkness as in a mirror. The " emphasis " or colour of Light alone came to the Darkness; the Light itself merely looked at it and

withdrew without taking any part of the Darkness. But from the Light the Darkness took a view and the " emphasis " or colour of matter; therefore it was displeasing to the Light. Although, therefore, the more evil took from the better not the true Light, but a certain appearance and " emphasis " of light, it acquired it by a forcible alteration of the good. Therefore there is no perfect good in this world, and what there is is very slight because that which was conceived originally was very small. But through this slight portion of Light, or rather through the appearance of Light, the creatures were able to produce a likeness related to that mixture which they had conceived from the Light. And this is the creation which we know by experience.

HEGEMONIUS, *Acta Archelai* lxvii. 5, 7-11;
cf. John 1: 5.

(3) What I mean is that those who undergo the so-called tribulations have really sinned unawares and by those other failings are brought to this good thing. They are accused because of the goodness of their leader but actually on other grounds, so that they may not suffer as men condemned for confessed crimes, nor be reproached like an adulterer or murderer but because they are not yet Christians though born such by nature.* He will console them so that they will not even seem to suffer. If anyone who has not sinned at all comes to suffer, such a case is rare; and he will not suffer from the plotting of power. He will suffer as the infant suffered who seems not to have sinned.

(4) The infant has not previously or actively sinned at all, but within himself he has the potentiality of sinning. When he is subjected to suffering he is benefited even though he reaps many unpleasant results. Just so, even if a perfect man has not sinned in act or by chance but suffers, his suffering corresponds to that of the infant. For within himself he has the capacity for sin, even though, since he did not accept the opportunity to sin, he did not sin. Therefore his not sinning

*Reading with K. Holl, *Epiphanius*, I (Leipzig, 1915), 262.

is no credit to him. The man who wants to commit adultery is an adulterer even if he does not happen to commit adultery; the man who wants to commit murder is a murderer even if he is unable to murder [cf. Matt. 5: 22, 28]. Similarly if I see the suffering of anyone whom I may call sinless, I shall call his will to sin even if he has done nothing evil. For I will say anything rather than call Providence evil.

(5) Now if you disregard all these arguments and try to put me to shame by using certain examples, perhaps saying that so and so did not sin but he did suffer—if you permit me, I will say that he did not sin but was like the infant who suffers. And if you should force out my argument more violently, I will say that any man you may name is a man; the just one is God [Mark 10: 18; Luke 18: 19]. For " no one," as someone said, " is pure from defilement " [Job. 14: 4].

CLEMENT, *Strom.* iv. 81-83;
from the 23rd book of *Exegetica*;
the last section deals with the martyrdom of Jesus.

(6) The apostle said, " I once lived apart from law " [Rom. 7: 9]—that is, before I came into this body I lived in that kind of body which was not under law, such as that of an animal or a bird.

ORIGEN, *Comm. in Rom.* v. 1.

(7) We suppose that one part of the so-called will of God is to love all things, because all things preserve a relation to the whole; another is to desire nothing; a third is to hate nothing.

CLEMENT, *Strom.* iv. 86. 1.

(8) Basilides and Isidore [the legitimate son and disciple of Basilides] say that Matthias told them secret words which he had heard from the Saviour in private instruction.

HIPPOLYTUS, *Ref.* vii. 20. 1.

(9) Basilides was taught by Glaukias, the " interpreter " of Peter.

CLEMENT, *Strom.* vii. 106. 4.

3

Isidore, Son of Basilides

A. ON THE INSEPARABLE SOUL

If you persuade anyone that the soul is not indivisible but that the passions of the wicked come from the force of the " appendages,"* worthless men are given no slight pretext for saying, " I was forced, I was carried away, I did it unwillingly, I acted against my will." But the man himself is the leader of his desire for evil things and does not fight against the force of the " appendages." We must acquire superiority by our reasoning faculty and show ourselves masters of the inferior creation [cf. Gen. 1: 28] within us.

CLEMENT, *Strom.* ii. 113. 4-114. 1.

B. EXPOSITIONS OF THE PROPHET PARCHOR

The Attics say that certain matters were intimated to Socrates by an attendant spirit [*daimon*]. And Aristotle says that all men are provided with spirits which attend them while they are in the body. He takes this teaching from the prophets and transfers it to his own books without acknowledging the source of the statement. . . . No one should suppose that what we call peculiar to the elect was spoken previously by any of the

* Cf. Marcus Aurelius *Med.* 12, 3, 4, genuinely Stoic according to W. Theiler, *Kaiser Marc Aurel; Wege zu sich selbst,* Zurich, 1951, 345.

philosophers. For it was not their discovery; they appropriated it from the prophets and attributed it to some " wise man "— who according to them does not exist. . . . It seems to me that those who philosophise do so in order to learn what the " winged oak " is, and what the " cloak embroidered on it " is—all of which Pherecydes used as theological allegories after taking the idea from the prophecy of Ham.

CLEMENT, Strom. vi. 53. 3-5.

C. ETHICS

When the apostles asked whether it was better not to marry, the Lord answered, " Not all can keep this saying, for some are eunuchs from birth, others from necessity " [Matt. 19: 11-12]. Some have a natural aversion to women from birth, and they make right use of this natural constitution by not marrying. These are the eunuchs " from birth." Those " from necessity " are continent for the sake of theatrical contests; they control themselves because of the attraction given by approval. These, then, become eunuchs in accordance with necessity, not reason. But those who make themselves eunuchs because of the eternal kingdom choose this course because of the consequences of marriage, fearing that they will lack leisure [cf. 1 Cor. 7: 5] because they will have to earn money.

The apostle said, " It is better to marry than to burn " [1 Cor. 7: 9], lest you cast your soul into fire while you resist night and day and are afraid of falling away from continence; while the soul resists it is separated from hope.

Therefore avoid a " contentious woman " [Prov. 21: 9, 19] so that you will not be torn away from the grace of God. After emitting the seed of " fire," pray with a good conscience. But when your prayer of thanksgiving declines into petition, and you ask for the future not to be reformed but to fall, then marry. But if someone is a youth or a pauper or is impotent, and he does not wish to marry in accordance with this word, he must not be separated from his brother. He is to say, " I have entered into the Holy of Holies, and I cannot experience passion." But if he has a suspicion [that he may fall], he is to say, " Brother, lay your hand on me, so that I will not sin." He will receive aid in mind and sense. He must only wish to attain what is good, and he will attain it.

Sometimes we say with our mouth, " We do not wish to sin, but the notion of sin is in my mind." Such a person does not do what he wishes simply because of fear that punishment will be put to his account. But mankind has certain needs which are both necessary and natural, others which are only natural.* The need of clothing is necessary and natural, while the need of sexual intercourse is natural but not necessary.

CLEMENT, Strom. iii. 1-3.

* Cf. Epicurea, frag. 456 Usener.

PART V

VALENTINUS AND HIS SCHOOL

Until very recently all that was preserved from Valentinus' writings consisted of fragments of letters and homilies and a psalm. His system could be recovered to some extent from Irenaeus, but it was hard to separate Valentinus from his follower Ptolemaeus. It could be known that he believed his system to be the product of revelation, for according to Hippolytus (Ref. vi. 42. 2) he said " that he saw a newborn infant and asked him who he was." The infant replied that he was the Logos. Valentinus then " added some tragic myth and wanted the heresy he was undertaking to consist of this." To analyse this experience is, of course, impossible. But it can be imagined that the Logos is the Logos of Jewish speculation and the Fourth Gospel (see the ' Gospel of Truth ' in Part V. 2) and that the " tragic myth " (Hippolytus' expression, used in derision) was not unlike the story found in the ' Secret Book of John ' (Part II 2).

In the ' Gospel of Truth,' Valentinus' primary concern is with the condition of the soul, though his cosmological doctrine lies in the background. The same concern is reflected in most of the fragments we translate in this section. Cosmology is prominent only in fragments 1 and 5.

In his ' Gnosis und spätantiker Geist ' II, 1 (1954) Jonas suggests that Valentinus is " demythologizing " the earlier Syrian cosmogonic gnosis. It is at least certain from the documents we have that the centre of his interest is different from that of the systems of Simon and Saturninus.

On Valentinus and Valentinianism cf. W. Foerster, ' Von Valentin zu Herakleon ' (*Giessen, 1928*); R. P. Casey, " *Two Notes on Valentinian Theology,*" ' *Harvard Theological Review* ' *23* (*1930*), *275-98;* G. Quispel, " *The Original Doctrine of Valentine,*" ' *Vigiliae Christianae* ' *1* (*1947*), *43-73;* F. M. Sagnard, ' *La gnose valentinienne et le témoignage de saint-Irénée* ' (*Paris, 1947*); G. Quispel, " *La conception de l'homme dans la gnose valentinienne,*" ' *Eranos-Jahrbücher* ' *15* (*1947*), *249-86;* R. A. Markus, " *Pleroma and Fulfilment,*" ' *Vigiliae Christianae* ' *8* (*1954*), *193-224.*

On the ' *Excerpts from Theodotus* '(*not given here*) *cf.* R. P. Casey, ' *The Excerpta ex Theodoto of Clement of Alexandria* ' (*London, 1935*); F. M. Sagnard, ' *Clement d'Alexandrie: Extraits de Théodote,*" (*Paris, 1949*); A. J. Festurgière, " *Notes sur les Extraits de Théodote,*" ' *Vigiliae Christianae* ' *3* (*1949*), *193-207.*

On names and formulae in the system *cf* H. Gressmann, " *Jüdisch-aramäisches bei Epiphanius,*" ' *Zeitschrift für die neutestamentliche Wissenschaft* ' *16* (*1915*), *191-97;* E. Peterson, " *Engel- und Dämonennamen. Nomina barbara,* " ' *Rheinisches Museum* ' *75* (*1926*), *394-421;* M. P. Nilsson, " *Sophia-Prunikos,*" ' *Eranos* ' *45* (*1947*), *169-72.*

Letters and Homilies (fragments)

A. LETTERS (FRAGMENTS)

(1) Something like fear of this creature [man] fell upon the
angels, for he made utterances greater than were suitable for
his creation, because of the One who had invisibly put in him
the seed of the substance from above—the One who expresses
himself freely. So also among the generations of earthly men,
the works of men become terrors to those who make them, as
in the case of statues and images and everything which
[human] hands fashion in the name of a god. So Adam,
having been fashioned in the name of a man, inspired the fear
attaching to the pre-existent Man, as if this Man had his
existence in him. The angels were terrified and rapidly
marred the work.

CLEMENT, Strom. ii. 36. 2-4

(2) The Good is one [Matt. 19: 17]. His presence is the
manifestation through the Son. By him alone can the heart
become pure [Matt. 5: 8], when every evil spirit is expelled
from the heart. For many spirits dwelling in it do not allow
it to be pure; each one of them performs its own works, insult-
ing it in many ways with unseemly desires. To me it seems
that the heart suffers rather as an inn does. An inn [cf. Plato,
Rep. 580a] has holes and trenches made in it and often is
filled with dung by men who stay there with licentious be-
haviour and take no care of the place since it belongs to some-

one else. Just so, the heart is unclean before it is cared for; it is the abode of many demons. But when the Father, who alone is good, visits it, it is sanctified and shines with light. Thus he who has such a heart is " blessed, because he will see God " [Matt. 5: 8].

CLEMENT, *Strom.* ii. 114. 3-6

(3) While enduring everything he was continent. Jesus exercised his divine nature. He ate and drank in a peculiar way [cf. Matt. 11: 19] and did not evacuate his food. For he had so great a power of continence that the food was not corrupted in him, since he himself was not perishable.

CLEMENT, *Strom.* iii. 59. 3

B. HOMILIES (FRAGMENTS)

(4) From the very beginning you are immortal and children of eternal life. You wished to distribute death among yourselves in order to consume it and spend it, so that death might die in you and through you. For when you destroy the world but are not destroyed yourselves, you are lords over the creation [cf. Gen. 1: 28] and over all decay.

CLEMENT, *Strom.* iv. 89. 1-3

(5) The world is as much inferior to the living Aeon as the image is to the living person. What, then, is the cause of the image? It is the greatness of the person who provides the example for the painter, so that it may be honoured by his [the person's] name. For even though the authenticity of the form is not found [in the image], the name fills up what is lacking in the work. The invisible power of God works with [the creation] so that we believe that the creation is his.

CLEMENT, *Strom.* iv. 89. 6-90. 1

(6) Many things written in the ordinary books are also written in the church of God. For they are common words from the heart, the law written in the heart [Jer. 31: 33].

This is the people of the Beloved, loved by him and loving him.

CLEMENT, Strom. vi. 52. 3-4

(7)   " *Harvest* "

In spirit I see all things suspended;
In spirit I perceive all things borne up;
Flesh suspended from soul,
Soul borne up by air,
Air hanging from ether,
Out of the deep, fruits being borne,
Out of the womb, a child is borne.

HIPPOLYTUS, Ref. vi. 37. 7

2

The Gospel of Truth

Irenaeus and Tertullian tell us that the Valentinians made use of a ' Gospel of Truth' different from the four canonical gospels accepted by the church. In modern times, however, their gospel remained completely unknown until the discovery of the Nag-Hammadi papyri in 1945 or 1946, and the probable identification of this particular work several years later. The book was published in 1956 in an edition produced by M. Malinine, H.-C. Puech, and G. Quispel (' Evangelium Veritatis,' Zurich). Four pages were missing, but these have turned up among the photographic reproductions from another Nag-Hammadi codex published by P. Labib (' Coptic Gnostic Papyri,' Cairo, 1956); these were identified by H. M. Schenke in ' Theologische Literaturzeitung,' 83 (1958), 497-500, and translated into German. Cf. also K. Grobel, ' The Gospel of Truth,' New York 1960. H. M. Schenke (' Die Herkunft des sogenannten Evangelium Veritatis' Berlin, 1958) disputes its Gnostic origin.

The translation which follows has been made from the Coptic text provided by Malinine, Puech, and Quispel, and—for the " missing " four pages—from the photographs of Labib.

The gospel of truth is joy to those who have received from the Father of truth the gift of knowing him by the power of the Logos, who has come from the pleroma [and] who is in the thought and the mind of the Father; he it is who is called " the Saviour," since that is the name of the work which he must do for the redemption of those who have not known the Father. For the name [of] the gospel is the manifestation of hope,

146

since that is the discovery of those who seek him, because the all sought for him from whom it had come forth. You see, the all had been inside of him, that illimitable, inconceivable one, who is better than every thought [16: 31-17: 9].

This ignorance of the Father brought about terror and fear. And terror became dense like a fog, that no one was able to see. Because of this, error became strong. But it worked on its hylic substance vainly, because it did not know the truth. It was in a fashioned form while it was preparing, in power and in beauty, the equivalent of truth. This, then, was not a humiliation for him, that illimitable, inconceivable one. For they were as nothing, this terror and this forgetfulness and this figure of falsehood, whereas this established truth is unchanging, unperturbed [and] completely beautiful [17: 9-27].

For this reason, do not take error too seriously. Thus, since it had no root, it was in a fog as regards the Father, engaged in preparing works and forgetfulnesses and fears in order, by these means, to beguile those of the middle and to make them captive. The forgetfulness of error was not revealed. It did not become [light] beside the Father. Forgetfulness did not exist with the Father, although it existed because of him.* What exists in him is knowledge, which was revealed so that forgetfulness might be destroyed and that they might know the Father. Since forgetfulness existed because they did not know the Father, if they then come to know the Father, from that moment on forgetfulness will cease to exist [17: 28-18: 11].

That is the gospel of him whom they seek, which he has revealed to the perfect through the mercies of the Father [as] the hidden mystery, Jesus the Christ. Through him he enlightened those who were in darkness because of forgetfulness. He enlightened them [and] gave [them] a path. And that path is the truth which he taught them. For this reason error was angry with him, [so] it persecuted him. It was distressed by him, [so] it made him powerless.† He was nailed to a cross. He became a fruit of the knowledge of the Father. He

* Or, " if it existed, then (it existed) because of him."
† Or, " (so) it crushed him," or " wore him down."

did not, however, destroy [them] because they ate of it. He rather caused those who ate of it to be joyful because of this discovery [18: 11-29].

And as for him, them he found in himself, and him they found in themselves, that illimitable, inconceivable one, that perfect Father who made the all, in whom the all is, and whom the all lacks, since he retained in himself their perfection, which he had not given to the all. The Father was not jealous. What jealousy, indeed, is there between him and his members? For, even if the Aeon had [received] their [perfection], they would not have been able to approach [the perfection of] the Father, because he retained their perfection in himself, giving it to them as [a way to re]turn to him and as a knowledge unique in perfection. He is the one who set the all in order and in whom the all existed and whom the all lacked. As one of whom some have no knowledge, he desires that they know him and that they love him. For what is it that the all lacked, if not the knowledge of the Father? [18: 29-19: 17]

He became a guide, quiet and at leisure. In the middle of a school he came [and] spoke the word, as a teacher. Those who were wise in their own estimation came to put him to the test. But he discredited them as empty-headed people. They hated him because they really were not wise men. After all these came also the little children, those who possess the knowledge of the Father. When they became strong they were taught the aspects of the Father's face. They came to know [and] they were known. They were glorified [and] they gave glory. In their heart, the living book of the living was manifest, [the book] which was written in the thought and in the mind [of the] Father and, from before the foundation of the all, is in that incomprehensible part of him [19: 17-20: 3].

This is [the book] which no one found possible to take, since it was reserved for him who will take it and be slain. No one was able to be manifest from those who believed in salvation as long as that book had not appeared. For this reason, the compassionate, faithful Jesus was patient in his sufferings until he took that book, since he knew that his death meant life for many. Just as in the case of a will which has not yet been opened, the fortune of the deceased master of the house is hidden, so also in the case of the all which had been hidden as long as the Father of the all was invisible [and] unique in himself, in whom every space has its source. For this reason Jesus appeared. He took that book as his own. He was nailed to a cross. He affixed the edict of the Father to the cross [20: 3-27].

Oh, such great teaching! He abases himself even unto death, though he is clothed in eternal life. Having divested himself of these perishable rags, he clothed himself in incorruptibility, which no one could possibly take from him. Having entered into the empty territory of fears, he passed before those who were stripped by forgetfulness, being both knowledge and perfection, proclaiming the things that are in the heart [of the Father], so that [he became the] wisdom of those who have [received] instruction.* But those who are to be taught, the living who are inscribed in the book of the living, learn for themselves, receiving instructions from the Father, turning to him again [20: 27-21: 8].

Since the perfection of the all is in the Father, it is necessary for the all to ascend to him. Therefore, if one has knowledge, he gets what belongs to him and draws it to himself. For he who is ignorant, is deficient, and it is a great deficiency, since he lacks that which will make him perfect. Since the perfection of the all is in the Father, it is necessary for the all to ascend to him and for each one to get the things which are his. He registered them first, having prepared them† to be given to those who came from him [21: 8-25].

Those whose name he knew first were called last, so that [the] one who has knowledge is he whose name the Father has pronounced. For he whose name has not been spoken is ignorant. Indeed, how shall one hear if his name has not been uttered. For he who remains ignorant until the end is a

---

* Or, "who are without instruction." The lacuna is of such a nature that it affords both possibilities, opposites though they may be.
† I.e., "the things which are his."

creature of forgetfulness and will perish with it. If this is not
so, why have these wretches no name, [why] do they have no
sound? Hence, if one has knowledge, he is from above. If
he is called, he hears, he replies and he turns towards him
who called him and he ascends to him and knows what he is
called. Since he has knowledge, he does the will of him who
called him. He desires to please him and he finds rest. He
receives a certain name.* He who thus is going to have
knowledge knows whence he came and whither he is going.
He knows it as a person who, having become intoxicated, has
turned from his drunkenness and having come to himself, has
restored what is his own [21: 25-22: 20].

He has turned many from error. He went before them to
their own places, from which they departed when they erred
because of the depth of him who surrounds every place,
whereas there is nothing which surrounds him. It was a great
wonder that they were in the Father without knowing him
and that they were able to leave on their own, since they were
not able to contain him and know him in whom they were,
for indeed his will had not come forth from him. For he
revealed it as a knowledge with which all its emanations†
agree, namely, the knowledge of the living book which he
revealed to the Aeons at last as his [letters], displaying to them
that these are not [merely] vowels nor consonants,‡ so that
one may read them and think of something void of meaning;
on the contrary, they are letters which convey the truth.
They [the letters] are pronounced only when they are known.
Each letter is a perfect truth like a perfect book, for they are
letters written by the hand of the unity, since the Father wrote
them for the Aeons, so that they by means of his letters might
come to know the Father [22: 20-23: 18].

While his wisdom meditates on the logos, [and] since his
teaching expresses it, his knowledge has been revealed. His
honour [?] is a crown upon it. Since his joy agrees with it,

* Lit., " the name of an individual comes to be his."
† The meaning of the Coptic word is unknown.
‡ Lit., " these are not images of voices nor are they letters which do not lack
a voice."

his glory exalted it. It has revealed his image. It has obtained
his rest. His love took bodily form around it. His trust embraced it. Thus the logos of the Father goes forth into the all,
being the fruit of his heart and expression of his will. It sup-
ports the all. It chooses and also takes the form of the all,
purifying it* and causing it to return to the Father [and] to
the Mother, Jesus of the utmost† sweetness. The Father opens
his bosom, but his bosom is the Holy Spirit. He reveals his
hidden self [his hidden self is his son], so that through the
compassion of the Father the Aeons may know him, end their
wearying search for the Father‡ [and] rest themselves in him,
knowing that this is rest: after he had filled what was incomplete, he did away with form. The form of it [i.e., what was
incomplete] is the world, that which it served. For where
there is envy and strife, there is an incompleteness. But where
there is unity, there is completeness. Since this incompleteness came about because they did not know the Father, so
when they know the Father, incompleteness, from that moment
on, will cease to exist. As one's ignorance disappears when he
gains knowledge, [and] as darkness disappears when light
appears, so also incompleteness is eliminated by completeness.
Certainly, from that moment on, form is no longer manifest,
but will be dissolved in fusion with unity [for now their works
lie scattered]. In time unity will make the spaces complete.
By means of unity each one will understand itself. By means
of knowledge it will purify itself of diversity [with a view]
towards unity, devouring matter within itself like fire and
darkness by light, death by life [23: 18-25: 19].

Certainly, if these things have happened to each one of us,
it is fitting for us, surely, to think about the all so that the
house may be holy and silent for unity. Like people who
have moved from a neighbourhood,§ if they have some dishes
around which are not good, they usually break them. Never-

---

* Plural, " them," in text.
† " Last, final, utmost." No need to negativise the adjective to read " limitless,
boundless."
‡ Lit., " and cease being weary (and) seeking after the Father."
§ Lit., " some places."

theless the householder does not suffer a loss, but rejoices, for
in the place of these defective dishes there are those which are
completely perfect. For this is the judgment which has come
from above and which has judged every person, a drawn two-
edged sword cutting on this side and that. When it appeared,
I mean, the Logos, who is in the heart of those who pronounce it—it was not merely a sound but it has become a
body—a great disturbance occurred among the dishes, for
some were emptied, others filled; some were provided for,
others were removed; some were purified, still others were
broken. All the spaces were shaken and disturbed for they
had no composure nor stability. Error was disturbed [?], not
knowing what it should do. It was troubled, it lamented, it
was beside itself because it did not know anything. When
knowledge, which is its abolishment, approached it with all
its emanations, error is empty, since there is nothing in it.
Truth appeared; all its emanations recognised it. They
actually greeted the Father with a power which is complete
[and] which joins them with the Father. For each one loves
truth because truth is the mouth of the Father. His tongue is
the Holy Spirit, who joins him to truth, attaching him to the
mouth of the Father by his tongue [at the time] he shall
receive the Holy Spirit [25: 19-27: 4].

This is the manifestation of the Father and his revelation
to his Aeons. He revealed his hidden self* and explained it.
For who is it who exists if it is not the Father himself. All the
spaces are his emanations. They knew that they stem from
him as children from a perfect man. They knew that they had
not yet received form nor had they yet received a name,
every one of which the Father produces. If they at that time
receive form of his knowledge, though they are truly in him,
they do not know him. But the Father is perfect. He knows
every space which is within him. If he pleases, he reveals
anyone whom he desires by giving him a form and by giving
him a name; and he does give him a name and cause him to
come into being. Those who do not yet exist are ignorant of

* Lit., " that of him which is hidden."

him who created them. I do not say, then, that those who do
not yet exist are nothing. But they are in him who will desire
that they exist when he pleases, like the event which is going
to happen. On the one hand, he knows, before anything is
revealed, what he will produce. On the other hand, the fruit
which has not yet been revealed does not know anything, nor
is anything either. Thus each space which, on its part, is in
the Father comes from the existent one, who, on his part, has
established it from the non-existent. For he who has no root
has no fruit, but thinks to himself: " I have become . . ."*;
he will be destroyed by it. For this reason, he who does not
exist at all, will never exist [27: 5-28: 24].

What, then, is that which he wants him to think? " I am
like the shadows and phantoms of the night." When morning
comes, this one knows that the fear which he had experienced
was nothing. Thus they were ignorant of the Father; he is
the one whom they did not see. Since there had been fear
and confusion and a lack of confidence and double-minded-
ness and division, there were many illusions which were con-
ceived† by him, the foregoing, as well as empty ignorance—
as if they were fast asleep and found themselves a prey to
troubled dreams: Either there is a place to which they flee, or
they lack strength as they come, having pursued unspecified
things: either they are involved in inflicting blows, or they
themselves receive bruises; either they are falling from high
places, or they fly off through the air, though they have no
wings at all.‡ Other times it is as if certain people were trying
to kill them, even though there is no one pursuing them; or,
they themselves are killing those beside them, for they are
stained by their blood. Until the moment when they who are
passing through all these things—I mean they who have
experienced all these confusions—awake, they see nothing
because they [the dreams] were nothing. It is thus that they
who cast ignorance from them as sheep do not consider it to
be anything, nor regard its properties to be something real,

* The Coptic letters are unclear at this crucial point.
† Lit., " done."   ‡ Lit., " there are no wings there at all."

but they renounce them like a dream in the night and they consider the knowledge of the Father to be the dawn. It is thus that each one has acted, as if he were asleep, during the time when he was ignorant and thus he comes to understand, as if he were awakening. And happy is the man who comes to himself and awakens. Indeed, blessed is he who has opened the eyes of the blind [28: 24-30: 16].

And the Spirit came to him in haste when it raised him. Having given its hand to the one lying prone on the ground, it placed him firmly on his feet, for he had not yet stood up. He gave them the means of knowing the knowledge of the Father and the revelation of his son. For when they saw it and listened to it, he permitted them to take a taste of and to smell and to grasp the beloved son [30: 16-32].

He appeared, informing them of the Father, the illimitable one. He inspired them with that which is in the mind, while doing his will. Many received the light and turned towards him. But material men were alien to him and did not discern his appearance nor recognise him. For he came in the likeness of flesh and nothing blocked his way because it was incorruptible and unrestrainable. Moreover, while saying new things, speaking about what is in the heart of the Father, he proclaimed the faultless word. Light spoke through his mouth, and his voice brought forth life. He gave them thought and understanding and mercy and salvation and the Spirit of strength derived from the limitlessness of the Father and sweetness. He caused punishments and scourgings to cease, for it was they which caused many in need of mercy to astray from him in error and in chains—and he mightily destroyed them and derided them with knowledge. He became a path for those who went astray and knowledge for those who were ignorant, a discovery for those who sought, and a support for those who tremble, a purity for those who were defiled [30: 32-31: 35].

He is the shepherd who left behind the ninety-nine sheep which had not strayed and went in search of that one which was lost. He rejoiced when he had found it. For ninety-nine is a number of the left hand, which holds it. The moment he finds the one, however, the whole number is transferred to the right hand. Thus it is with him who lacks the one, that is, the entire right hand which attracts that in which it is deficient, seizes it from the left side and transfers it to the right. In this way, then, the number becomes one hundred. This number signifies the Father.* [31 : 35-32 : 17]

He laboured even on the Sabbath for the sheep which he found fallen into the pit. He saved the life of that sheep, bringing it up from the pit in order that you may understand fully what that Sabbath is, you who possess full understanding.† It is a day in which it is not fitting that salvation be idle, so that you may speak of that heavenly day which has no night and of the sun which does not set because it is perfect. Say then in your heart that you are this perfect day and that in you the light which does not fail dwells [32 : 18-34].

Speak concerning the truth to those who seek it and of knowledge to those who, in their error, have committed sins. Make sure-footed those who stumble and stretch forth your hands to the sick. Nourish the hungry and set at ease those who are troubled. Foster men who love. Raise up and awaken those who sleep. For you are this understanding which encourages.‡ If the strong follows this course, he is even stronger. Turn your attention to yourselves. Do not be concerned with other things, namely, that which you have cast forth from yourselves, that which you have dismissed. Do not return to them to eat them. Do not be moth-eaten. Do not be worm-eaten, for you have already shaken it off. Do not be a place of the devil, for you have already destroyed him. Do not strengthen your last obstacles, because that is reprehensible. For the lawless one is nothing. He harms himself more than the law. For that one does his works because he is a lawless person. But this one, because he is a righteous person, does his

---

* Lit., " the sign of that which is their sound is: this is the Father."

† Lit., "You are the children of the understanding of the heart." For the order cf. W. Till in *Orientalia* 27 (1958), 178.

‡ The Coptic word means basically " pluck, draw," but the context seems to require the verb to mean " inspire, encourage, strengthen," as one might do in stretching forth one's hand to the sick, etc.

works among others. Do the will of the Father, then, for you are from him [32: 35-33: 32].

For the Father is sweet and his will is good. He knows the things that are yours, so that you may rest yourselves in them. For by the fruits one knows the things that are yours, that they are the children of the Father, [and one knows] his aroma, that you originate from the grace of his countenance. For this reason, the Father loved his aroma; and it manifests itself in every place; and when it is mixed with matter, he gives his aroma to the light; and into his rest he causes it to ascend in every form [and] in every sound. For there are no nostrils* which smell the aroma, but it is the Spirit which possesses the sense of smell and it draws it for itself to itself and sinks into the aroma of the Father. He is, indeed, the place for it, and he takes it to the place from which it has come, in the first aroma which is cold. It is something in a psychic form, resembling cold water which is . . .† since it is in soil which is not hard, of which those who see it think, " It is earth." Afterwards, it becomes soft again. If a breath is taken, it is usually hot. The cold aromas, then, are from the division. For this reason, God came and destroyed the division and he brought the hot pleroma of love, so that the cold may not return, but the unity of the perfect thought prevail [33: 33-34: 34].

This is the word of the Gospel of the finding of the pleroma for those who wait for the salvation which comes from above. When their hope, for which they are waiting, is waiting—they whose likeness is the light in which there is no shadow, then at that time the pleroma is about to come. The deficiency of matter, however, is not because of the limitlessness of the Father who comes at the time of the deficiency. And yet no one is able to say that the incorruptible One will come in this manner. But the depth of the Father is increasing, and the thought of error is not with him. It is a matter of falling down

---

* We expect here not *ear*, but *nose*. The transposition of several Coptic letters of the word meaning *ear*—a type of mistake common among copyists—gives us the word meaning *nostrils*.

† The meaning of the Coptic verb is unknown.

[and] a matter of being readily set upright at the finding of that one who has come to him who will turn back [34: 34-35: 22].

For this turning back is called "repentance." For this reason, incorruption has breathed. It followed him who has sinned in order that he may find rest. For forgiveness is that which remains for the light in the deficiency, the word of the pleroma. For the physician hurries to the place in which there is sickness, because that is the desire which he has. He [the sick man] is in a deficient condition, but he does not hide himself, because he [the physician] possesses that which he lacks. In this manner the deficiency is filled by the pleroma, which has no deficiency, which has given itself out in order to fill the one who is deficient, so that grace may take him, then, from the area which is deficient and has no grace. Because of this a diminishing occurred in the place where there is no grace, the area where the one who is small, who is deficient, is taken hold of [35: 22-36: 9].

He revealed himself as a pleroma, i.e., the finding of the light of truth which has shined towards him, because he is unchangeable. For this reason, they who have been troubled speak about Christ in their midst so that they may receive a return and he may anoint them with the ointment. The ointment is the pity of the Father, who will have mercy on them. But those whom he has anointed are those who are perfect. For the filled vessels are those which are customarily used for anointing. But when an anointing is finished, it [the vessel] is usually empty, and the cause for its deficiency is the consumption of its ointment. For then a breath is drawn only through the power which he has. But the one who is without deficiency—one does not trust anyone beside him nor does one pour anything out. But that which is deficient is filled again by the perfect Father. He is good. He knows his plantings because he is the one who has planted them in his paradise. And his paradise is his place of rest [36: 10-39].

This is the perfection in the thought of the Father and these are the words of his reflection. Each one of his words is the work of his will alone, in the revelation of his Logos.

Since they were in the depth of his mind, the Logos, who was the first to come forth, caused them to appear, along with an intellect which speaks the unique word by means of a silent grace. It was called " thought," since they were in it before becoming manifest. It happened, then, that it was the first to come forth—at the moment pleasing to the will of him who desired it; and it is in the will that the Father is at rest and with which he is pleased. Nothing happens without him, nor does anything occur without the will of the Father. But his will is incomprehensible. His will is his mark,* but no one can know it, nor is it possible for them to concentrate on it in order to possess it. But that which he wishes takes place† at the moment he wishes it—even if the view does not please anyone: it is God's will.‡ For the Father knows the beginning of them all as well as their end. For when their end arrives, he will question them to their faces. The end, you see, is the recognition of him who is hidden, that is, the Father, from whom the beginning came forth [and] to whom will return all who have come from him. For they were made manifest for the glory and the joy of his name [36: 39-38: 6].

And the name of the Father is the son. It is he who, in the beginning, gave [a] name to him who came forth from him—he is the same one—and he begat him for a son. He gave him his name which belonged to him—He, the Father, who possesses everything which exists around him. He possesses the name; he has the son. It is possible for them to see him. The name, however, is invisible, for it alone is the mystery of the invisible about to come to ears completely filled with it through his [the Father's] agency. Moreover, as for the Father, his name is not pronounced, but it is revealed through a son. Thus, then, the name is great [38: 6-24].

Who, then, has been able to pronounce [a] name for him, this great name, except him alone to whom the name belongs and the sons of the name in whom the name of the Father is

---

* Lit., " footstep."
† Lit., " is (there)."
‡ Lit., " in the presence of God, the will."

at rest, [and who] themselves in turn are at rest in his name, since the Father has no beginning?* It is he alone who engendered it for himself as a name in the beginning before he had created the Aeons, that the name of the Father should be over their heads as a lord—that is, the real name, which is secure by his authority [and] by [his] perfect power. For the name is not drawn from lexicons nor is his name derived from common name-giving. But it is invisible. He gave a name to himself alone, because he alone saw it [and] because he alone was capable of giving himself a name. For he who does not exist has no name. For what name would one give him who did not exist? Nevertheless, he who exists also with his name and he alone knows it, and to him alone the Father gave a name. The son is his name. He did not, therefore, keep it secretly hidden, but the son came into existence. He himself gave a name [to him]. The name, then, is that of the Father, just as the name of the Father is the son, For otherwise, where would compassion find a name—outside of the Father? But someone will probably say to his companion, " Who would give a name to someone who existed before himself, as if, indeed, children did not receive their name from one of those who gave them birth? " [38: 25-40: 2].

Above all, then, it is fitting for us to think this point over: What is the name? It is the real name. It is, indeed, the name which came from the Father, for it is he who owns the name. He did not, you see, get the name on loan, as in the case of others because of the form in which each one of them is going to be created. This, then, is the authoritative name. There is no one else to whom he has given it. But it remained unnamed, unuttered, till the moment when he, who is perfect, pronounced it himself; and it was he [alone] who was able to pronounce his name and to see it. When it pleased him, then, that his son should be his pronounced name and [when] he gave this name to him, he who has come from the depth spoke of his secrets, because he knew that the Father was

---

* That is, he is one who did not come into existence, because he has always been in existence.

absolute goodness.* For this reason, indeed, he sent this [particular] one in order that he might speak concerning the place and his place† of rest from which he had come forth, and that he might glorify the pleroma, the greatness of his name and the sweetness of the Father [40: 2-41: 3].

Each one will speak concerning the place from which he has come forth, and to the region from which he received his essential being, he will hasten to return once again. And he went from that place—the place where he was—because he tasted of that place, as he was nourished and grew. And his own place of rest is his pleroma. All the emanations from the Father, therefore, are pleromas, and all his emanations have their roots in the one who caused them all to grow from himself. He appointed a limit. They, then, became manifest individually in order that [they] might be in their own thought, for that place to which they extend their thought is their root, which lifts them upwards through all heights to the Father. They reach‡ his head, which is rest for them, and they remain there near to it so that they say that they have participated in his face by means of embraces. But these of this kind were not manifest, because they have not risen above themselves. Neither have they been deprived of the glory of the Father nor have they thought of him as small, nor bitter, nor angry, but as absolutely good, unperturbed, sweet, knowing all the spaces before they came into existence and having no need of instruction. Such are they who possess from above [something] of this immeasurable greatness, as they strain towards that unique and perfect one who exists there for them. And they do not go down to Hades. They have neither envy nor moaning, nor is death in them. But they rest in him who rests, without wearying themselves or becoming involved in the search for truth. But they, indeed, are the truth, and the Father is in them, and they are in the Father, since they are perfect, inseparable from him who is truly good. They lack nothing

---

* Lit., " free of sin."
† Perhaps *hendiadys*: " concerning his place of rest."
‡ Lit., " they have."

in any way, but they are given rest [and] are refreshed by the Spirit. And they listen to their root; they have leisure for themselves, they in whom he will find his root, and he will suffer no loss to his soul [41: 3-42: 37].

Such is the place of the blessed; this is their place. As for the rest, then, may they know, in their place, that it does not suit me, after having been in the place of rest to say anything more. But he is the one in whom I shall be in order to devote myself, at all times, to the Father of the all and the true brothers, those upon whom the love of the Father is lavished, and in whose midst nothing of him is lacking. It is they who manifest themselves truly since they are in that true and eternal life and speak of the perfect light filled with the seed of the Father, and which is in his heart and in the pleroma, while his Spirit rejoices in it and glorifies him in whom it was, because he [the Father] is good. And his children are perfect and worthy of his name, because he is the Father. Children of this kind are those whom he loves [42: 37-43: 24].

W. W. ISENBERG

Note to Chapters 3-5

Ptolemaeus was the head of the Valentinian school in Italy and apparently succeeded Valentinus himself, perhaps about 160. Nothing is known of his life, but it is evident from his work that he was the greatest systematic theologian of the school. Irenaeus' refutation of Valentinianism is directed primarily against that form of it created by Ptolemaeus, and our description of the system is translated from Irenaeus, ' Adv. haer.' i. 1-8 (I, 8-71 Harvey).

He was also an exegete, indeed the first exegete of the Fourth Gospel known to us. In the selection provided, once more, by Irenaeus (' Adv. haer.' i. 8. 5; I, 75-80 Harvey), he tried to prove that John, the Lord's disciple, knew and allegorically described the first Ogdoad in the prologue to his gospel.

And he was an apologist for Valentinianism. In his ' Letter to Flora' he set forth the answers to some theological difficulties encountered by a Christian woman named Flora, carefully leading her along a seemingly orthodox path to the point where she will recognise that the Valentinians share in the apostolic tradition and that the truth of their teaching is guaranteed by the words of the Saviour. This letter is preserved by Epiphanius, ' Pan. haer.' xxxiii. 3-7; we translate the text of G. Quispel, ' Ptolémée: Lettre à Flora ' (Paris, 1949). " Flora " may be the Roman Church; see ' Vigiliae Christianae ' 11 (1957), 147-48.

3

The Valentinian System of Ptolemaeus

A. THE PLEROMA

(1. 1)* There is a perfect pre-existent Aeon, dwelling in the invisible and unnameable elevations; this is Pre-Beginning and Forefather and Depth. He is uncontainable and invisible, eternal and ungenerated, in quiet and in deep solitude for infinite aeons. With him is Thought, which is also called Grace and Silence. Once upon a time, Depth thought of emitting from himself a Beginning of all, like a seed, and he deposited this projected emission, as in a womb, in that Silence who is with him. Silence received this seed and became pregnant and bore Mind, which resembled and was equal to him who emitted him. Mind alone comprehends the magnitude of his Father; he is called Only-Begotten and Father and Beginning of all. Along with him, Truth was emitted; this makes the first Four, the root of all: Depth and Silence, then Mind and Truth.

When Only-Begotten perceived why he had been emitted, he too emitted Logos and Life, since he was the Father of all who were to come after him and was the beginning and form of the whole Pleroma. From the union of Logos and Life were emitted Man and Church. This is the originative Eight,

---

* These numbers refer to chapters and sections in Irenaeus as divided by Massuet and printed in Harvey's text.

the root and substance of all, called by four names: Depth and
Mind and Logos and Man. Each of them is male-female, as
follows: first the Forefather was united with his own Thought;
then Only-Begotten [Mind] with Truth; then Logos with Life
and Man with Church.

(2) When these Aeons, which had been emitted to the
glory of the Father, themselves desired to glorify the Father
through their own products, they emitted emanations by
uniting. After emitting Man and Church, Logos and Life
emitted ten other Aeons, whose names are as follows: Deep
and Mingling, Unageing and Union, Self-Produced and
Pleasure, Immovable and Mixture, Only-Begotten and Blessing. Man with Church emitted twelve Aeons, whose names
are as follows: Paraclete and Faith, Paternal and Hope,
Maternal and Love, Everlasting and Intelligence, Ecclesiastical
and Blessedness, Willed and Sophia. (3) These are the thirty
Aeons which are kept in silence and are not known. This is
the invisible and spiritual Pleroma, triply divided into an
Eight, a Ten, and a Twelve.

Proofs from Scripture

For this reason the Saviour* did nothing openly for thirty
years [cf. Luke 3: 23], in order to set forth the mystery of these
Aeons. In the parable of the labourers in the vineyard [Matt.
20: 1-16] there is a very clear indication of these thirty Aeons,
for labourers are sent about the first hour, others about the
third, others about the sixth, others about the ninth, and others
about the eleventh and when these hours are added together
they make the sum of thirty—for $1+3+6+9+11=30$. The
hours mean Aeons. These are the great and marvellous and
ineffable mysteries which we bear as fruit.

* Irenaeus adds that the Valentinians do not wish to call the Saviour " Lord."

B. DISTURBANCE AND RESTORATION
IN THE PLEROMA

(2. 1) The Forefather was known only to Only-Begotten Mind], who came into existence from him, while to all the rest he is invisible and incomprehensible. Only Mind took pleasure in beholding the Father and rejoiced in understanding his immeasurable magnitude. Mind intended to impart to the other Aeons the magnitude of the Father, to tell them his greatness and his size and how he was without beginning and uncontainable and incapable of being seen; but Silence, by the Father's will, restrained him because she wished to lead all of them to the thought and longing of seeking for their Forefather. Likewise the other Aeons silently longed to see the one who had emitted their seed and to learn of the root without beginning.

(2) It was the very last and youngest of the Twelve derived from Man and Church, the Aeon Sophia, which leaped forth [cf. Wisd. 18: 15] and experienced passion apart from the embrace of her consort Willed. That [longing] which started at those about Mind and Truth fell suddenly on this erring Aeon, on the pretext of love but actually because of audacity, because she did not have fellowship with the perfect Father such as Mind enjoyed. Her passion was the search for the Father; for she wished to comprehend his magnitude. When she was unable to do so, because she had undertaken an impossible task and was in great agony because of the greatness of the depth and the inscrutability of the Father [cf. Rom. 11: 33] and her love for him, she was ever extended forward, so that she would finally have been swallowed up by his sweetness and dissolved into the substance of the whole [Pleroma] if she had not encountered the power which consolidates all [the Aeons] and keeps them outside the Ineffable Magnitude. This power is called Limit. By it Sophia was stopped and consolidated and—with difficulty—made to return to herself [cf. Luke 15: 17]; and since she was persuaded that the

Father is incomprehensible, she put off her former Desire along with the passion which had come upon her when she was struck by wonder.

Another Valentinian Version

(3) Since Sophia had undertaken an impossible and unattainable task, she brought forth a shapeless being, a thing such as a female [by herself] can bear. When she looked at it, she first grieved because of the imperfection of the creature; then she was afraid that it would cease to be; then she was amazed and at a loss, as she sought for its cause and wondered how to hide what had come into existence. While she was concerned with her passions, she obtained conversion and tried to run upwards to the Father; she came to such a point of daring that she became exhausted and became a suppliant of the Father. The other Aeons, especially Mind, also made petition with her. From this the substance of matter had its primal origin, from her ignorance and grief and fear and consternation. (4) In addition to the others, the Father through Only-Begotten emitted Limit in his own image [cf. Gen. 1:26], without companion, without female.*

C. THE WORK OF LIMIT: THE
RESTORATION OF SOPHIA

Limit is also called Cross and Redeemer and Emancipator and Definer and Guide. Through Limit Sophia was purified and consolidated and restored to union with her partner. For when Desire had been separated from her, along with the passion which had come upon her, she herself remained within the Pleroma, but her Desire, with the passion, was separated and crucified [cf. Gal. 6:14]† by Limit. When Desire was outside Limit, it was a spiritual substance, like some natural

---

* Irenaeus adds that "sometimes the Father is said to be accompanied by Silence and sometimes the Valentinians say he is beyond male and beyond female."

† Cf. also Ignatius, *Rom.* vii. 2: "my *eros* has been crucified."

desire of an Aeon, but it was shapeless and ugly because it comprehended nothing. Therefore it was a weak female fruit.

(5) After Desire had been banished outside the Pleroma of the Aeons, its [her] Mother was restored to her own partner, while Only-Begotten again emitted another pair in accordance with the Father's foreknowledge so that none of the Aeons might experience passion as Sophia did. This pair was Christ and Holy Spirit, emitted from the fixity and consolidation of the Pleroma; by these the Aeons were made perfect. For Christ taught them the nature of pairs [cf. Matt. 19: 6] and that they were capable of comprehending the ungenerated one (?), and he proclaimed among them the knowledge [*epignosis*] of the Father—how he is uncontainable and incomprehensible and cannot be seen or heard, but is known only through Only-Begotten [John 1: 18]. The cause of the eternal permanence of the other [Aeons] is what in the Father is incomprehensible; that of the origin and formation is what in the Father is comprehensible, his Son. The Christ who had just been emitted effected these things in them.

(6) When they had all been made equal, Holy Spirit taught them to give thanks and explained what the true "rest" [cf. Gen. 2: 2; Heb. 4: 10] was. Thus the Aeons became equal in form and in mind, becoming all Minds, all Logoi, all Men, all Christs; similarly all the female Aeons became Truths and Lives and Spirits and Churches.* After this, all things were consolidated and given perfect rest; with great joy they praised the Forefather and shared in much gladness. And because of this beneficence, the whole Pleroma of the Aeons with one counsel and mind [while Christ and Spirit consented and their Father ratified the decision]—each one of the Aeons gave and contributed what it had that was most beautiful and bright—wove together and united their contributions harmoniously, and emitted an emanation to the honour and glory of Depth. This was the most perfect beauty and the star of the Pleroma, its perfect fruit, Jesus, who is also called Saviour and Christ and Logos, after his origin, and All,

* So Irenaeus; the system requires the order " Churches and Spirits."

because he is from all [cf. Col. 2: 9]. As guards for him they emitted angels of the same kind as themselves.

Proofs from Scripture

(3. 1) These matters were not described openly because not all hold this knowledge (*gnosis*) [Matt. 19: 11], but were all spoken mysteriously through parables by the Saviour to those who were able to understand in this way [Matt. 13: 10-11]. ... Paul very clearly names these Aeons at many points and also preserves their order, for he says, "To all the generations of the Aeons of the Aeon" [Eph. 3: 21]. When members of the psychic Church end prayers of thanksgiving with "to the Aeons of the Aeons," they are referring to those Aeons [above]. (2) The emanation of the Twelve of Aeons is signified by the Saviour's discourse with the scribes at the age of twelve [Luke 2: 42] and by his choice of the apostles; for there were twelve apostles. The other eighteen Aeons are indicated in his eighteen months' stay with the disciples after the resurrection of the dead, as well as through the first two letters of his name, *iota* [10] and *eta* [8].* The ten Aeons are signified by the first letter of his name, (*iota*); therefore the Saviour said, "One *iota* or one apex shall not pass away until everything takes place" [Matt. 5:18]. (3) The passion which was experienced in relation to the twelfth Aeon is indicated through the apostasy of Judas, who was the twelfth of the apostles [cf. Mark 3: 19, etc.], and through the fact that he [the Saviour] suffered in the twelfth month; for he proclaimed the gospel for one year after his baptism. Furthermore, this is most clearly revealed in the case of the woman with an issue of blood [Matt. 9: 20-22, etc.]. She had suffered for twelve years before she was healed by the coming of the Saviour, when she touched the hem of his garment, and therefore the Saviour said, "Who touched me?"—teaching the disciples the mystery which had taken place among the Aeons and the healing of the Aeon which had experienced passion. For

* The same exegesis of *iota* and *eta* is found in Barnabas ix. 8 and elsewhere in early Christian literature, but without reference to the Aeons.

the one who suffered for twelve years is that power which would have been extended and whose substance would have flown into the boundless [cf. Luke 8: 43 var., " had spent all her living "], unless she had touched the garment of the Son, that is, of the Truth of the first Four [indicated through the " hem "] and she would have been dissolved into the general substance. But she stayed there and stopped experiencing passion, for the power of the Son which came forth [i.e., Limit] healed her and separated the passion from her.

(4) The Saviour, who is from all, is the All because of the expression, " All, a male, which opens the womb " [Luke 2: 23]; he, being the All, opened the womb of the Desire of the suffering Aeon [Sophia] and banished it [Desire] outside the Pleroma; this Desire is the second Eight. For this reason Paul plainly said, " And he is the All " [Col. 3: 11], and again, " All is to him and from him is All " [Rom. 11: 36], and again, " In him dwells All, the Pleroma of deity " [Col. 2: 9], and " All is recapitulated in Christ through God " [Eph. 1: 10].

(5) Limit has two modes of operation, confirming and dividing. As he confirms and strengthens, he is Cross; so when he divides and delimits, he is Limit. The Saviour thus indicated his modes of operation: first the confirming, when he said, " Whoever does not bear his Cross and follow me cannot be my disciple " [Luke 14: 27; Mark 10: 38], and again, " Take up the Cross and follow me " [Mark 8: 34]; the delimiting, when he said, " I came not to cast peace but a sword " [Matt. 10: 34]. And John indicated the same thing when he said, " The fan is in his hand; he will purify the threshing-floor and will gather the wheat into his barn; but he will burn up the chaff in unquenchable fire " [Luke 3: 17]. In this saying he indicated the operation of Limit; for that " fan " is the Cross, which is actually consuming all the material elements as fire consumes chaff but is purifying those who are saved as the fan purifies wheat. Paul the apostle himself referred to this Cross in the following words: " The message of the Cross is folly to those who are perishing but the power

of God to those who are saved "[1 Cor. 1: 18], and again,
" Far be it from me to boast of anything except the Cross of
Christ, through which the world has been crucified to me and
I to the world " [Gal. 6: 14].

D. DESIRE [ACHAMOTH] AND THE
DEMIURGE OUTSIDE THE PLEROMA

(4. 1) When the Desire of the Sophia above, also called
Achamoth,* had been banished from the Pleroma above, by
necessity she was cast with her passion in places of Shadow and
the Void. She was outside the Light and the Pleroma; she was
shapeless and ugly, like an abortion, because she had comprehended onthing. The Christ above took pity on her and was extended through the Cross to form her shape by his own power, a
shape which was in substance only, not in knowledge. When
he had done this, he returned above, withdrawing his power,
and left her, so that she might sense the passion related to her
because of her departure from the Pleroma and might strive
for better things, since she had a certain aroma of imperishability which had been left her by Christ and the Holy Spirit.
For this reason she is called by both names, Sophia after her
mother† [for her mother was called Sophia] and Holy Spirit
from the Spirit with Christ.

When she received shape and became intelligent, and was
immediately deprived of the Logos which had invisibly been
with her [i.e., Christ], she strove to seek for the light which
had left her; but she was unable to comprehend it [cf. John
1: 5] because she was hindered by Limit. Then the Limit
which was hindering her in her forward striving said, " Iao."
This is the origin of the name Iao.

Since she was unable to pass through Limit because she was
entangled with passion and had been abandoned outside, she
was weighed down by every part of passion [which was multi-

---

* The lower Sophia thus bears a name like the Hebrew word for " wisdom."
† Irenaeus says " father," ironically (cf. Sagnard, 163).

partite and manifold]. She suffered grief, because she did not comprehend; fear, lest life abandon her as light had done; in addition to these, perplexity; all these, in ignorance. She was not like her mother, the First Sophia Aeon, who had degeneration in her passions; on the contrary, another disposition came upon her, that of conversion to the Life-Giver.

(2) This was the composition and substance of the matter of which the universe consists. From the conversion [of Achamoth] the whole soul of the universe and of the Demiurge originated; from her fear and grief the rest took their origin.

For from her tears comes every humid substance, from her laughter that which shines with light; from her grief and consternation come the corporeal elements of the universe.

> Sometimes she mourned and grieved,
>> For she was left alone in darkness and the void;
> Sometimes she reached a thought of the light which
>> had left her,
>> And she was cheered and laughed;
> Sometimes she feared;
>> At other times she was perplexed and astonished.*

(5) Our Mother passed through every passion and barely emerged from them, she turned to supplicate the light which had left her, i.e., Christ. When he had ascended to the Pleroma, he sent the Paraclete to her, i.e., the Saviour, having given him all the power of the Father [cf. Matt. 28: 18] and having delivered everything under his authority. The Aeons similarly so that "in him all things might be created, visible and invisible, thrones, deities, dominions" [cf. Col. 1: 16]. He was sent out to her along with the angels who were his peers.

When Achamoth turned towards him she was at first ashamed and put on a veil, but then when she saw him with his whole harvest [of angels] she ran to him and received power from his appearing.

* Cf. the Naassene hymn, page 115.

He gave her the formation which is in accordance with knowledge and providing healing for her passions; he separated them from her but did not neglect them [for it was not possible for them to vanish as the passions of the prior Sophia did, since they were habitual and powerful]. After separating them he mixed them together and solidified them and changed them from incorporeal passion into incorporeal matter. Then he provided them with an aptitude and a nature so that they could become compounds and bodies, so that there might be two natures, the one from the passions evil, the other from the conversion in a state of emotion. In this way the Saviour practically effected a work of creation.

When Achamoth was relieved of passion, and joyfully conceived the vision of the lights with him [i.e., the angels with him] and in her longing became pregnant with fruits after their image, a spiritual embryo after the likeness of the guards of the Saviour.

(5. 1) When these three kinds of materials existed—matter from passion, the psychic from conversion, the spiritual which she conceived—she turned to shaping them. But she was unable to shape the spiritual since it was of the same nature as she was. She turned then to shaping the psychic nature which had come into existence from her conversion and projected the teachings of the Saviour. First, from the psychic nature she formed the Father and King of all who are of the same nature as he is [i.e., the psychics]—which are on the right hand— and of those who come from passion and matter—which are on the left hand. He shaped all the beings after himself, secretly moved by the Mother; hence he is called Mother- Father and Fatherless and Demiurge and Father. He is Father of those on the right [i.e., the psychics], he is Demiurge of those on the left [i.e., material beings]; and he is King of them all. Desire [Achamoth] wanted to make all things in honour of the Aeons and she made images of them—or rather the Saviour did so through her. And she preserved the image of the invisible Father, which was not known by the Demiurge; the Demiurge preserved that of the Only-Begotten Son; the

archangels and angels made by him preserved the images of the other Aeons.

(2) The Demiurge was the Father and God of the beings outside the Pleroma, the maker of all psychic and material beings. For he separated the two mixed natures, and made bodies out of the incorporeal, and thus created heavenly and earthly beings, and became the Demiurge of material and psychic beings, the right and the left, the light and the heavy, those borne above and those borne below. He fashioned seven heavens and dwells above them. For this reason he is called Seven, and the Mother Achamoth is called Eight; she preserves the number of the first-generated Eight, the first in the Pleroma. The seven heavens are intelligent; they are angels, and the Demiurge himself is an angel, like God. Paradise, which is above the third heaven [cf. 2 Cor. 12: 2, 4] is practically an archangel, and from him Adam received something when he lived in him.

(3) The Demiurge supposed that he made these things of himself, but he made them after Achamoth projected them. He made heaven without knowing heaven; he formed man in ignorance of man; he brought earth to light without understanding earth. In every case he was ignorant of the ideas of the things he made, as well as of the Mother; and he thought he was entirely alone. But the Mother was the cause of his creating; she wanted to bring him forth as the head and beginning of her own nature and as lord of the whole operation. The Mother is called Eight and Sophia and Earth and Jerusalem and Holy Spirit and Lord [in her masculine aspect]; she has the place of the Middle and is above the Demiurge but below or outside the Pleroma, until the end.

(4) Since, then, the material nature is derived from the three passions, fear and grief and perplexity, psychic beings consist of fear and conversion; the Demiurge originated from conversion, and all the rest of the psychic creation—souls of irrational animals and beasts and men—comes from fear. For this reason the Demiurge, who is impotent to know spiritual beings, thought that he was the only God and said through

the prophets, " I am God and apart from me there is no one " [Is. 45: 5, 46: 9]. From grief came " the spiritual beings of wickedness " [Eph. 6: 12], as well as the Devil, also called World-Ruler, and the demons and the angels and all the spiritual substance of wickedness. The Demiurge is the psychic son of our Mother, while the World-Ruler is the creation of the Demiurge. The World-Ruler knows the beings above him, for he is a spirit of wickedness, but the Demiurge does not know them since he is merely psychic. Our Mother dwells in the superheavenly place, i.e., in the Middle, while the Demiurge dwells in the heavenly place, i.e., in the Seven, and the World-Ruler in our universe.

From perplexity and anguish, as from a very ignoble source, came the corporeal elements of the universe—earth related to the stability of consternation, water related to the motion of fear, air related to the congelation of grief. Fire is immanent in all of them as death and decay, just as ignorance is hidden in the three passions.

(5) When he had fashioned the universe, he made the earthly man, not out of this dry land but out of the invisible substance, taking him from the liquid and flowing part of matter; and into him was breathed the psychic [man]. This is the man who came into being " after the image and likeness " [Gen. 1: 26]; " after the image " is the material, who is similar to God but not of the same substance; " after the likeness " is the psychic, and his substance is therefore called " spirit of life " [Gen. 2: 7] since it is from spiritual emanation. Finally he was clothed with the " coat of skin " [Gen. 3: 21]; this is his flesh which is subject to sense-perception.

(6) The embryo of our Mother Achamoth, which she conceived in accordance with the vision of the angels about the Saviour [it is of the same spiritual substance as that of the Mother], was unknown to the Demiurge and was secretly inserted into him while he remained ignorant, so that through him it might be sown into the soul created by him and into the material body, might grow and increase in them, and might become ready for the reception of the perfect Logos.

The Demiurge was unaware of the spiritual man who was sown, in his "inbreathing" [Gen. 2: 7], by Sophia with ineffable power and foreknowledge. As he did not know the Mother, so he does not know her seed. This seed is the Church, which corresponds to the [Aeon] Church above. Man thus has his soul from the Demiurge, his body from liquid and his flesh from matter, but his "spiritual man" from the Mother Achamoth.

E. SALVATION

(6. 1) There are these three elements in man: the material, also called "left," which necessarily perishes since it cannot possibly receive the breath of imperishability; the psychic, also called "right," which lies between the spiritual and the material and extends to either one as it has the inclination; the spiritual, which was sent forth to be shaped in union with the psychic and to be instructed with it in its conduct. This [last element] is the "salt" and the "light of the world" [Matt. 5: 13-14]; for it needed psychic and perceptible instructions; for this reason the universe was constructed. And the Saviour came to this psychic element, since it has free will, in order to save it. He assumed the primary elements of those beings which he was going to save. •From Achamoth he took the spiritual, from the Demiurge he put on the psychic Christ, and from the constitution of the universe he acquired a body which had psychic substance and was constructed by ineffable art so to be visible, tangible, and subject to passion. He acquired nothing material at all, for matter is not capable of being saved. The end will come when all that is spiritual is shaped and perfected in knowledge. All that is spiritual means the spiritual men who have perfect knowledge about God and have been initiated in the mysteries of Achamoth.

(2) The psychic men have been instructed in psychic matters; they are strengthened by works and mere faith and do not have the perfect knowledge; they belong to the

[earthly] church. Good conduct is necessary for them, for otherwise they cannot be saved; but we [spirituals] shall certainly be saved not by conduct but simply because we are by nature spiritual. Just as the earthly cannot participate in salvation, for it is not capable of receiving it [cf. 1 Cor. 15: 50], so in turn the spiritual cannot accept decay, no matter what actions it undertakes. Just as gold placed in mud does not lose its beauty but retains its own nature, and the mud cannot harm the gold, so we cannot damage or lose our spiritual nature, even if we engage in various material actions.*

(4) Those of the church receive grace as a loan, and therefore will be deprived of it; but we have it as our own possession after it has come down from above from the ineffable and unnameable Pair. For this reason it will be " bestowed " on us [cf. Matt. 6: 33; Luke 19: 26], and we must always meditate on the mystery of union in every way. Whoever is " in the world " and does not love a woman so that he unites with her is not " of the truth " and will not attain the truth; but he who is from the world and unites with a woman will not attain the truth because he lustfully unites with the woman. For this reason the psychics, who are " of the world," [John 17: 11, 14-16; 18: 37] must practise continence and good conduct, so that through it they may come to the place of the Middle; for us, who are spiritual and perfect, this is not necessary at all. It is not conduct which leads one to the Pleroma, but the seed sent out from there as an infant and made mature [perfect] there:

(7. 1) When the whole seed is perfected, then our Mother Achamoth will depart from the place of the Middle and will enter into the Pleroma and will receive the Saviour [made from all the Aeons] as her bridegroom, so that there will be a union of the Saviour and the Sophia who is Achamoth. These are the bridegroom and the bride [cf. John 3: 29], and the bridechamber is the whole Pleroma.

* (6, 3) At this point Irenaeus criticises the Valentinians for eating meat consecrated to pagan gods, for attending pagan festivals and gladiatorial shows, and for seducing women. (6, 4) They also despise ordinary Christians for their ignorance, while regarding themselves as " perfect " and " seeds of election."

The spirituals will put off their souls and will become intelligent spirits, entering without hindrance, and invisibly, into the Pleroma, and they will be given as brides to the angels about the Saviour. The Demiurge himself will depart to the place of the Mother Sophia, in the Middle, and the souls of the righteous too will be refreshed in the place of the Middle, for nothing psychic can come within the Pleroma. When these events take place, then the fire hidden in the universe will shine forth and ignite and become effective in consuming all matter along with itself and finally will become non-existent. The Demiurge knew none of these things before the coming of the Saviour.

(2) The Demiurge, some say, emitted Christ, his own son, a psychic being like him, and spoke concerning him through the prophets. He passed through Mary as water passes through a pipe. On him at the baptism there descended that Saviour from the Pleroma, from all [the Aeons], in the form of a dove. The Saviour was a composite being consisting of these four elements and thus preserving the model of the primal and original Four—from the spiritual what was from Achamoth; from the psychic, what was from the Demiurge; from the constitution of the universe, what was constructed by ineffable art; and from the Saviour, what was the dove which came down into him. It (the Saviour) remained impassible—for it could not experience passion, since it was unconquerable and invisible—therefore when he (Christ) was led before Pilate, that Spirit of Christ set in him was taken away. But the seed which was from the Mother also did not experience passion, for it too was impassible because it was spiritual and invisible, even to the Demiurge. What suffered was the psychic Christ, the one constructed from the constitution of the universe, in a mysterious fashion, so that through him the Mother might set forth the model of the Christ above, when he was extended on the cross and had shaped the essential form of Achamoth.*

* This paragraph is from another system as Irenaeus indicated.

F. REVELATION

(7. 3) The souls which have the seed of Achamoth are better than the others, and therefore are loved more by the Demiurge, who does not know why he loves them but supposes that they are what they are because they come from him. For this reason he appointed them as prophets, priests, and kings. Many statements were made by this seed through the prophets .... since its nature is highly exalted; and the Mother spoke many things concerning things above, but she did so through it [the seed] and the souls originating from it. The prophecies contain three kinds of statements: those which stem from the Mother; those which stem from the seed; those which stem from the Demiurge. Similarly the sayings of Jesus were derived partly from the Saviour, partly from the Mother, and partly from the Demiurge.

(4) Since the Demiurge was ignorant of what was above him, he was moved by what was said but thought little of it, attributing various causes to it, such as the prophetic spirit, which has some movement of its own, or the man [who was speaking], or his involvement in inferior matters. Thus he continued in ignorance until the coming of the Saviour; but when the Saviour came he learned everything from him and gladly joined him, with all his power. He is the centurion in the gospel [Matt. 8: 9; Luke 7: 8], who said to the Saviour, " I too have under my authority soldiers and slaves, and they do whatever I command "; he will govern the structure of the universe until the appointed time, especially because of his care for the church and his knowledge of the reward prepared for him, his going to the place of the Mother.

(5) There are three classes of men: spiritual, material, psychic, corresponding to Cain, Abel, and Seth, who reflect these three natures not as individuals but generically. The material ends in decay; and the psychic, if it chooses what is better, will rest in the place of the Middle; if it chooses what is worse, it too will end in a destiny like its choice. Whatever

spiritual beings Achamoth inseminates in righteous souls, even until now, trained and brought up here [on earth], because they were sent forth as infants, were later accounted worthy of maturity [perfection] and will be given as brides to the angels of the Saviour, while their souls will be forced to rest for ever in the Middle with the Demiurge. These souls themselves are divided into those by nature good and those by nature evil; the good are those which are capable of receiving the seed; those by nature evil can never receive that seed.

G. BIBLICAL PROOFS

(8. 2) In the last times of the universe the Saviour came to his passion for this reason: to set forth the passion which took place in regard to the last of the Aeons, and through this end [of life] to show the goal of the operation of the Aeons. That twelve-year-old girl, the daughter of the head of the synagogue [Luke 8: 41], whom the Saviour stood by and raised from the dead, corresponds to Achamoth, whom the extended Christ shaped and led to perception of the light which had left her. Because the Saviour manifested himself to her when she was outside the Pleroma [as was right for an abortion], Paul said in First Corinthians [15: 8], " Last of all he appeared also to me as to the abortion." The coming of the Saviour and his peers [angels] to Achamoth was also revealed by Paul in the same epistle [11: 10] when he said, " The woman must have a veil on her head because of the angels." The fact that, when the Saviour came to her, Achamoth placed a veil over her face for shame, was also made manifest by Moses when he placed a veil over his face [cf. 2 Cor. 3: 13].

The passions of Achamoth were indicated by the Saviour on the cross. When he said, " My God, why have you abandoned me? " [Matt. 27: 46; Mark 15: 34] he indicated that Sophia had been abandoned by the light and kept by Limit from moving forward. Her grief was shown by " My soul is grieved " [Matt. 26: 38]; her fear in the saying,

" Father, if it be possible, let the cup pass from me " [Matt. 26: 39]; and her perplexity in the statement, " And I do not know what to say " [John 12: 27].

(3) He also pointed out the three kinds of men: (1) the material, when he answered the one who said he would follow him by saying, " The Son of Man has nowhere to lay his head " [Matt. 8: 20; Luke 9: 58]; (2) the psychic, when he answered the one who said he would follow him but first had to arrange his affairs, " No one who lays his hand on the plough and then looks back is ready for use in the kingdom of heaven " [Luke 9: 62]—this person is one of those of the Middle, and he has acted like the one who has acknowledged most parts of righteousness but then does not wish to follow but has been overcome by riches so that he does not become perfect [Matt. 19: 16], and he has become one of the psychic class; and (3) the spiritual, when he said, " Let the dead bury their own dead " [Matt. 8: 22; Luke 9: 60], and, in the case of Zacchaeus the tax collector, " Descend quickly, for I must stay in your house to-day " [Luke 19: 5]—these were men of the spiritual class. And the parable of the leaven, which the woman is said to have hidden in three measures of meal [Luke 13: 21], refers to the three classes; the woman is Sophia, the three measures of meal are the three classes of men [spiritual, psychic, earthly]; the leaven is the Saviour himself. And Paul explicitly spoke of earthly, psychic, and spiritual, in passages where he says " as is the earthly man, so are the earthly men " [1 Cor. 15: 48], " the psychic man does not accept the things of the Spirit " [1 Cor. 2: 14], and " the spiritual man judges everything " [1 Cor. 2: 15]. The passage, " The psychic man does not accept the things of the Spirit " was spoken in regard to the Demiurge, who, since he is psychic, did not know the Mother, since she is spiritual, or her seed, or the Aeons in the Pleroma. But Paul said that the Saviour received the first-fruits of those whom he was about to save: " If the first-fruit [or first beginning] is holy, so is the lump " [Rom. 11: 16]. By " first-fruit " he meant the spiritual, and by " lump " he meant members of the psychic church, the " lump " of which

he took up and raised up with himself, since he himself was " leaven."

(4) And that Achamoth wandered outside the Pleroma and was formed by Christ and was sought by the Saviour, he indicated when he said he came for the lost sheep [Matt. 18: 12; Luke 15: 3]. For the wandering sheep is our Mother from whom the church here was sown; her wandering is her life outside the Pleroma in all the passions from which matter came. The woman who cleans her house and finds the drachma [Luke 15: 8-9] is the Sophia above, who lost her Desire [Achamoth], and later finds it, when everything has been cleaned through the coming of the Saviour. For this reason she is restored within the Pleroma. And Simeon, who took the Christ in his arms and gave thanks to God, and said " Lord, now lettest thou thy servant depart in peace, according to thy word " [Luke 2: 28-29], is a figure of the Demiurge, who, when the Saviour came, learned of his change of place and gave thanks to Depth. And through Anna, the prophetess, who is proclaimed in the gospel, and had lived seven years with her husband, and for the remaining time had remained a widow, until she saw the Saviour and recognised him and spoke about him to all [Luke 2: 36-38]—she is very obviously Achamoth, who for a short time saw the Saviour with his peers [angels] but during the remaining interval waited in the Middle and " expected " his return, when he would restore her to her consort [Luke 2: 38]. And her name was indicated by the Saviour when he said, " And Sophia has been made righteous by her children " [Luke 7: 35], and by Paul thus: " We speak of Sophia among the perfect " [1 Cor. 2: 6]. And Paul spoke of the unions within the Pleroma, mentioning one example; for in writing of a human union he said, " This mystery is great, but I refer to Christ and the Church " [Eph. 5: 32].

4

Ptolemaeus' Exegesis of John

John the Lord's disciple, desiring to tell of the origin of the universe, by which the Father produced everything, posits a certain Beginning ["principle"] which was first generated by God, which he called Only-Begotten Son and God, in which the Father emitted all things spermatically. By this the Logos was emitted, and in it was the whole substance of the Aeons, which the Logos itself later shaped. Since, then, he speaks of the first origin, he rightly sets forth the teaching from the Beginning, i.e., God and the Logos; for he says, " In the Beginning was the Logos, and the Logos was with God, and the Logos was God; this was in the Beginning with God " [John 1: 1-2]. First he differentiates the three: God, Beginning, and Logos; then he combines them again in order to set forth the emission of each of them, the Son and the Logos, and their unity with each other and with the Father. For in the Father and from the Father is the Beginning, and in the Beginning and from the Beginning is the Logos. Rightly, then, he said, " In the Beginning was the Logos," for it was in the Son; and " the Logos was with God," for the Beginning was; and " the Logos was God," consequently, for what is generated of God is God [cf. John 3: 6]. " This was in the Beginning with God ": he set forth the order of emission. " All things came into existence through it, and apart from it nothing came into existence " [John 1: 3]: to all the Aeons after it the Logos was the cause of formation and origin. " What came into existence in it is Life" [John 1: 4]: from this he reveals the Pair (*syzygy*), for "all things" came into existence "through" it, but Life, "in" it. This, then, coming into existence *in* it, is closer *in* it than the things which came into existence *through* it; for it is present with it and bears fruit through it, since he adds, "And the Life was the Light of Men." Having just said "Man," he mentioned "Church" as having the same meaning as "Man," so that through the one name he might set forth the common nature of the Pair; for from Logos and Life come Man and Church. He spoke of Life as the Light of men because they are illuminated by it, i.e., transfigured and made manifest. This what Paul says [Eph. 5: 13]: "For everything made manifest is Light." Since, then, Life manifested and generated Man and Church, it is called their Light.

Clearly, then, through these words John explained [in addition to other matters] the second Tetrad: Logos and Life, Man and Church. Moreover, he revealed the first Tetrad. Discussing the subject of the Saviour, and saying that "everything" outside the Pleroma was formed through him, he says that he is the fruit of the whole Pleroma. For he called him the "Light shining in the Darkness and not overcome by it," since, even when he shaped everything which came into existence out of passion, he was not known by it. And he calls him Son and Truth and Life and Incarnate Logos, "whose glory we beheld, and his glory was such as belongs to the Only-Begotten, given him by the Father, full of Grace and Truth" [John 1: 14]. He speaks thus: "And the Logos became flesh and dwelt in us, and we beheld his glory, glory as of the Only-Begotten of the Father, full of Grace and Truth."

Correctly, then, he revealed the first Tetrad, mentioning Father and Grace and Only-Begotten and Truth. Thus John spoke about the first Ogdoad, the Mother of all the Aeons. For he spoke of Father and Grace and Only-Begotten and Truth and Logos and Life and Man and Church.

IRENAEUS, *Adv. haer.* i. 8. 5; I, 75-80 Harvey

5

Ptolemaeus' Letter to Flora

The Law ordained through Moses, my dear sister Flora, has not been understood by many persons, who have accurate knowledge neither of him who ordained it nor of its commandments. I think that this will be perfectly clear to you when you have learned the contradictory opinions about it.

Some say that it is legislation given by God the Father; others, taking the contrary course, maintain stubbornly that it was ordained by the opposite, the Devil who causes destruction, just as they attribute the fashioning of the world to him, saying that he is the Father and Maker of this universe. Both are completely in error; they refute each other and neither has reached the truth of the matter.

For it is evident that the Law was not ordained by the perfect God the Father, for it is secondary, being imperfect and in need of completion by another, containing commandments alien to the nature and thought of such a God. On the other hand, one cannot impute the Law to the injustice of the opposite [God], for it is opposed to injustice. Such persons do not comprehend what was said by the Saviour. " For a house or city divided against itself cannot stand " [Matt. 12: 25], declared our Saviour.

Furthermore, the apostle says that the creation of the world is due to him, for " everything was made through him and apart from him nothing was made " [John 1: 3]. Thus he takes away in advance the baseless wisdom of the false accusers, and shows that the creation is not due to a God who corrupts but to the one who is just and hates evil. Only unintelligent men have this idea, men who do not recognise the providence of the creator and have blinded not only the eye of the soul but also the eye of the body.

From what has been said, it is evident that these persons entirely miss the truth; each of the two groups has experienced this, the first because they do not know the God of justice, the second because they do not know the Father of all, who alone was revealed by him who alone came.

It remains for us who have been counted worthy of the knowledge of both of these to provide you with an accurate explanation of the nature of the Law and of the legislator by whom it was ordained. We shall draw the proofs of what we say from the words of the Saviour, which alone can lead us without error to the comprehension of reality.

First, you must learn that the entire Law contained in the Pentateuch of Moses was not ordained by one legislator— I mean, not by God alone; some commandments are his [Moses'] and some were given by men. The words of the Saviour teach us this triple division. The first part must be attributed to God himself and his legislating; the second to Moses [not in the sense that God legislates through him, but in the sense that Moses gave some legislation under the influence of his own ideas]; and the third to the elders of the people, who seem to have ordained some commandments of their own at the beginning. You will now learn how the truth of this theory is proved by the words of the Saviour.

In some discussion with those who disputed with the Saviour about divorce, which was permitted in the Law, he said, "Because of your hard-heartedness Moses permitted a man to divorce his wife; from the beginning it was not so; for God made this marriage, and what the Lord joined together, man must not separate" [Matt. 19: 8, 6]. In this way he shows that there is a Law of God, which prohibits the divorce of a wife from her husband, and another law, that of Moses, which permits the breaking of this yoke because of hard-

heartedness. In fact, Moses lays down legislation contrary to
that of God; for joining is contrary to not joining. But if we
examine the intention of Moses in giving this legislation, it
will be seen that he did not give it arbitrarily or of his own
accord, but by necessity because of the weakness of those for
whom the legislation was given. Since they were unable to
keep the intention of God, according to which it was not
lawful for them to reject their wives [with whom some of them
disliked to live], and therefore were in danger of turning to
greater injustice and thence to destruction, Moses wanted to
remove the cause of dislike, which was placing them in jeopardy
of destruction. Therefore because of the critical circumstances,
choosing a lesser evil in place of a greater, he ordained, of his
own accord, a second law, that of divorce, so that if they
could not observe the first, they might keep this and not turn
to unjust and evil actions, through which complete destruction
would be the result for them. This was his intention when he
gave legislation contrary to that of God. Therefore it is indis-
putable that here the law of Moses is different from the Law
of God, even if we have demonstrated the fact from only one
example.

The Saviour also makes plain the fact that there are some
traditions of the elders interwoven with the Law. " For God,"
he says, " said, Honour your father and your mother, that it
may be well with you. But you," he says, addressing the elders,
" have declared as a gift to God, that by which you might
have been aided by me; and you have nullified the Law of
God through the tradition of your elders." Isaiah also proclaimed this, saying, " This people honours me with their lips,
but their heart is far from me, teaching precepts which are the
commandments of men " [Matt. 15: 4-9].

Therefore it is obvious that the whole Law is divided into
three parts; we find in it the legislation of Moses, of the elders,
and of God himself. This division of the entire Law, as made
by us, has brought to light what is true in it. This part, the
Law of God himself, is in turn divided into three parts: the
pure legislation not mixed with evil, which is properly called

" law," which the Saviour came not to destroy but to complete [Matt. 5: 17]—for what he completed was not alien to him but needed completion, for it did not possess perfection; next the legislation interwoven with inferiority and injustice, which the Saviour destroyed because it was alien to his nature; and finally, the legislation which is exemplary and symbolic an image of what is spiritual and transcendent, which the Saviour transferred from the perceptible and phenomenal to the spiritual and invisible.

The Law of God, pure and not mixed with inferiority, is the Decalogue, those ten sayings engraved on two tablets, forbidding things not to be done and enjoining things to be done. These contain pure but imperfect legislation and required the completion made by the Saviour.

There is also the law interwoven with injustice, laid down for vengeance and the requital of previous injuries, ordaining that an eye should be cut out for an eye and a tooth for a tooth, and that a murder should be avenged by a murder. The person who is the second one to be unjust is no less unjust than the first; he simply changes the order of events while performing the same action. Admittedly this commandment was a just one and still is just, because of the weakness of those for whom the legislation was made so that they would not transgress the pure law. But it is alien to the nature and goodness of the Father of all. No doubt it was appropriate to the circumstances, or even necessary; for he who does not want one murder committed [saying, " You shall not kill "] and then commanded a murder to be repaid by another murder, has given a second law which enjoins two murders although he had forbidden one. This fact proves that he was unsuspectingly the victim of necessity. This is why, when his son came, he destroyed this part of the law while admitting that it came from God. He counts [this part of the law] as in the old religion, not only in other passages but also where he said, " God said, He who curses father or mother shall surely die " [Matt. 15: 4].

Finally, there is the exemplary part, ordained in the image

of spiritual and transcendent matters, I mean the part dealing with offerings and circumcision and the Sabbath and fasting and Passover and unleavened bread and other similar matters. Since all these things are images and symbols, when the truth was made manifest they were translated to another meaning. In their phenomenal appearance and their literal application they were destroyed, but in their spiritual meaning they were restored; the names remained the same but the content was changed. Thus the Saviour commanded us to make offerings not of irrational animals or of incense of this [worldly] sort, but of spiritual praise and glorification and thanksgiving and of sharing and well-doing with our neighbours. He wanted us to be circumcised, not in regard to our physical foreskin but in regard to our spiritual heart; to keep the Sabbath, for he wishes us to be idle in regard to evil works; to fast, not in physical fasting but in spiritual, in which there is abstinence from everything evil. Among us external fasting is also observed, since it can be advantageous to the soul if it is done reasonably, not for imitating others or from habit or because of a special day appointed for this purpose. It is also observed so that those who are not yet able to keep the true fast may have a reminder of it from the external fast. Similarly, Paul the apostle shows that the Passover and the unleavened bread are images when he says, "Christ our Passover has been sacrificed, in order that you may be unleavened bread, not containing leaven" [by leaven he here means evil] "but may be a new lump" [1 Cor. 5: 7].

Thus the Law of God itself is obviously divided into three parts. The first was completed by the Saviour, for the commandments, "You shall not kill, you shall not commit adultery, you shall not swear falsely," are included in the forbidding of anger, desire and swearing. The second part was entirely destroyed. For "an eye for an eye and a tooth for a tooth," interwoven with injustice and itself a work of injustice, was destroyed by the Saviour through its opposite. Opposites cancel out. "For I say to you, do not resist the evil man, but if anyone strikes you, turn the other cheek to him." Finally, there is the part translated and changed from the literal to the spiritual, this symbolic legislation which is an image of transcendent things. For the images and symbols which represent other things were good as long as the Truth had not come; but since the Truth has come, we must perform the actions of the Truth, not those of the image.

The disciples of the Saviour and the apostle Paul showed that this theory is true, speaking of the part dealing with images, as we have already said, in mentioning " the Passover for us " and the " unleavened bread "; of the law interwoven with injustice when he says that " the law of commandments in ordinances was destroyed " [Eph. 2: 15]; and of that not mixed with anything inferior when he says that " the Law is holy, and the commandment is holy and just and good " [Rom. 7: 12].

I think I have shown you sufficiently, as well as one can in brief compass, the addition of human legislation in the Law and the triple division of the Law of God itself.

It remains for us to say who this God is who ordained the Law; but I think this too has been shown you in what we have already said, if you have listened to it attentively. For if the Law was not ordained by the perfect God himself [as we have already taught you], nor by the devil [a statement one cannot possibly make], the legislator must be someone other than these two. In fact, he is the demiurge and maker of this universe and everything in it; and because he is essentially different from these two and is between them, he is rightly given the name " Intermediate."

And if the perfect God is good by nature, as in fact he is [for our Saviour declared that there is only a single good God, his Father whom he manifested]; and if the one who is of the opposite nature is evil and wicked, characterised by injustice; then the one situated between the two, neither good nor evil and unjust, can properly be called just, since he is the arbitrator of the justice which depends on him. On the one hand, this god will be inferior to the perfect God and lower than his justice, since he is generated and not ungenerated [there is

only one ungenerated Father, from whom are all things [cf.
I Cor. 8: 6], since all things depend on him in their own ways].
On the other hand, he will be greater and more powerful than
the adversary, by nature, since he has a substance and nature
different from the substance of either of them. The substance
of the adversary is corruption and darkness [for he is material
and complex], while the substance of the ungenerated Father
of all is incorruption and self-existent light, simple and homo-
geneous. The substance of the latter produced a double
power, while he [the Saviour] is an image of the greater one.

Do not let this trouble you for the present in your desire
to learn how from one first principle of all, simple, and acknowledged by us and believed by us, ungenerated and incorruptible and good, were constituted these natures of corruption
and the Middle, which are of different substances, although it
is characteristic of the good to generate and produce things
which are like itself and have the same substance. For, if God
permit, you will later learn about their origin and generation,
when you are judged worthy of the apostolic tradition which
we too have received by succession. We too are able to prove
all our points by the teaching of the Saviour.

In making these brief statements to you, my sister Flora,
I have not grown weary; and while I have treated the subject
with brevity, I have also discussed it sufficiently. These points
will be of great benefit to you in the future, if like fair and good
ground you have received fertile seeds and go on to show forth
their fruit.

EPIPHANIUS, *Pan.* xxxiii. 3-7

6

Marcosian Worship

Not very much is known about Valentinian cult practices; what we do know is told us by Irenaeus (' Adv. haer.' i. 13 and 21; I, 115-25 and 181-88 Harvey). He is describing, apparently from eye-witness accounts, what went on in the meetings of the Marcosians, followers of a Valentinian teacher named Marcus, who was active, perhaps in Gaul, in the latter half of the second century.

A. PROPHECY

(Marcus says to wealthy women): "I wish to share my Grace with you, since the Father of the All continually sees your angel before his face [cf. Matt. 18:10]. The Place of the Greatness is in us; we must achieve unity. Take Grace first from me and through me. Adorn yourself as a bride awaiting her bridegroom, so that you may be what I am and I may be what you are. Establish the seed of the light in your bride-chamber. Receive the bridegroom from me and contain him and be contained in him. Behold, Grace has descended upon you; open your mouth and prophesy." And when the woman replies, " I have never prophesied and I do not know how to prophesy," he makes some further invocations to astonish the deceived one, and says to her, " Open your mouth and say anything, and you will prophesy."

[The result is that she speaks nonsense, regards herself as a prophetess, and gives Marcus her property and person.]

IRENAEUS, *Adv. haer.* i. 13. 3; I, 118-19 Harvey

B. EUCHARIST

After preparing cups of mixed wine he greatly lengthens the prayer of invocation and makes them appear purple and red, so that the Grace from the powers above all may seem to pour drops of her blood into that cup through his invocation, and so that those who are present may have a strong desire to taste of that drink, by means of which the Grace may rain upon them. Again, he gives the women mixed cups and commands them to say the eucharistic prayer in his presence. When this has been done, he takes a cup larger than the one the woman has prayed over, and transfers the contents from the smaller one to his own, saying over it these words:

> May the Grace which is before all, inconceivable and ineffable, fill your " inner man " and increase knowledge of her in you, sowing in you the mustard seed in good earth.

After he has said these words the large cup is filled from the small one so that it overflows.

IRENAEUS, *Adv. haer.* i. 13. 2; I, 115-17 Harvey

C. BAPTISM

Some of them construct a bridal chamber and perform a mystical initiation with certain secret expressions for the initiates. They call this rite " spiritual marriage " in imitation of the unions above. Others lead candidates to water, and in baptizing them use this formula:

> Into the name of the unknown Father of all, into Truth

the mother of all, into him who came down into Jesus, into Unity and Redemption and Fellowship with the powers.

Others use certain Hebrew expressions.

In your name, Father! Be baptized in the Light in which the Spirit of Truth emanated for your redemption! May you live!

The one who has been initiated responds:

I have been anointed and I have been redeemed, and my soul has been redeemed from every Aeon, in the name of Iao, who redeemed his soul in the living Christ [or in Jesus the Nazarene]. . . .

Then those who are present say:

Peace be to all on whom this name rests.

Then they anoint the initiate with balsam gum, for they say that this ointment is a type of the sweet odour which is above all.

Some of them say that it is unnecessary to lead the initiate to water. They mix oil and water and pour the mixture on the head of the initiates, using formulas like those we have mentioned. They want this to be the redemption. They also anoint with balsam. . . .

D. EXTREME UNCTION

Others pour on the heads of dying persons a mixture of oil and water or of the previously mentioned unguent and water, so that they may become incomprehensible and invisible to the principalities and powers and so that their " inner man " may ascend invisibly above them, leaving their bodies behind in the creation, while their soul is left with the Demiurge. And they teach them to say, when they come to the powers after they are dead:

I am a Son from the Father, from the Father who was before, a Son in him who was before. I have come to see all things which are mine and not mine—not entirely alien, but they belong to Achamoth, who is female, and she made them for herself. I trace my origin to the pre-existent One, and I return to my own, whence I came.

They say that the one who says these things evades and escapes from the powers. When he comes to those which are about the Demiurge, he says to them:

I am a precious vessel, more precious than the female who made you. Your mother was ignorant of her origin, but I know mine; I know from whence I come, and I invoke the imperishable Sophia who is in the Father, the mother of your mother who has no father or husband. A female, daughter of a female, she made you in ignorance of her mother, thinking that she was alone. But I invoke her mother.

When those about the Demiurge hear these things, they are greatly troubled and recognise their origin and the origin of their mother; but the gnostic proceeds to his own, casting off his bond, i.e., the soul.

IRENAEUS, *Adv. haer.* i. 21. 3-5; I, 183-88 Harvey

7

Heracleon's Exegesis of John

*Like Ptolemaeus (Part V, 3-5), Heracleon belonged to the Italian
school of Valentinians. From Ptolemaeus we have exegesis of only the
first few verses of the Gospel of John (Part V, 4), but Heracleon composed exegetical notes on parts, at least, of the first eight chapters of the
Gospel. These notes are sometimes quoted by Origen in his 'Commentary on John,' written before and after his exile from Alexandria
in 231. They have been assembled by A. E. Brooke ('Texts and
Studies,' I, 4, Cambridge, 1891) and by W. Völker, 'Quellen zur
Geschichte der christlichen Gnosis' (Tübingen, 1932). The present
translation is revised from my earlier attempt in 'Second-Century
Christianity' (London, 1946), 39-52. The fragments are numbered
after Brooke and Völker, and where necessary the Johannine verse is
quoted first. Cf. also J. Mouson, " Jean-Baptiste dans les fragments
d'Héracléon," 'Ephemerides Theologicae Lovanienses,' 30 (1954),
301-22; Y. Janssens, " Héracléon," 'Le Muséon,' 72 (1959), 101-
51, 277-99.*

1. [John 1 : 3, " all things came into being through Him, and
outside Him nothing came into being."]   " All things "
means the world and what is in the world; the Aeon and what
is in the Aeon did not come into being through the Logos.
" Nothing," that is, of what is in the world and the creation.
The one who provided the cause of the generation of the world
to the Demiurge—and that one was the Logos—is not the one
" from whom " or " by whom " but the one " through whom."

For the Logos himself did not create as if he were given energy by another [so that " through him " might be understood thus] but, while he was giving energy, another created.

2. [John 1: 4, " in him was life."] " In him " means " for spiritual men," for he himself provided the first formation for them in accordance with their generation, producing and setting forth that which had been sown by another [so that it resulted] in form and illumination and individual outline.

3. [John 1: 18, " no one has ever seen God," etc.] This was said not by the Baptist but by the disciple [John].

4. [John 1: 21, " are you the prophet? "] John acknowledged that he was not the Christ or " a prophet " or " Elijah."

5. [John 1: 23, " I am a voice of one crying in the desert."] The Logos is the Saviour; the voice which was in the desert is that symbolised through John; and [its] echo is the whole prophetic order. The voice which is closely related to Logos [reason] becomes Logos [word], just as woman is transformed into man; and for the echo there will be a transformation into voice, giving the place of a disciple to the voice which changes into Logos, but the place of a slave to that which changes from echo into voice. When the Saviour calls him [John] " a prophet " and " Elijah " [Matt. 11: 9, 14] he does not teach his nature but his attributes; but when he calls him " greater than prophets " and " among those born of women " Matt. 11: 10-11], then he characterises John himself. When John himself is asked about himself, he does not answer about his attributes. Attributes are things like clothing, other than himself. When he was asked about his clothing, whether he himself were his clothing, would he have answered " Yes "?

[John 1: 19, " the Jews sent priests and Levites from Jerusalem to ask him."] It was the duty of these persons to investigate and inquire about these matters, since they were devoted to God; and John himself was of the Levitical tribe. They asked him if he were a prophet, since they wanted to learn about the general subject. " Greater " [than prophets, Matt. 11: 10; among those born of women, Matt. 11: 11] was prophesied by Isaiah, so that none of those who ever prophesied was deemed worthy of this honour by God.

6. [John 1:25, " why then do you baptize if you are not the Christ or Elijah or the prophet? "] Only Christ and Elijah and the prophets ought to baptize. The Pharisees asked the question from malice, not from a desire to learn.

7. [John 1:26, " I baptize in water."] John replies to those sent from the Pharisees, not in relation to their question, but on his own terms.

8. [John 1:26], " In your midst stands one whom you do not know."] This means that he is already present and is in the world and in men, and he is already manifest to all of you.

[John 1:27, " he comes after me, and I am not worthy to loose the thong of his sandal."] John is the forerunner of Christ. In these words the Baptist acknowledges that he is not worthy of even the least honourable service for Christ. " I am not worthy " that on my account he came down from the Greatness and assumed flesh as a sandal; of this flesh I cannot give an account or describe it or explain [unloose] the dispensation concerning it. The world is the sandal. [John represents the Demiurge.] The Demiurge of the world, who is inferior to Christ, acknowledges the fact through these expressions.

9. [John 1:28, " these things happened in Bethany across Jordan."] Heracleon read " Bethany " [Origen himself preferred " Bethabara "].

10. [John 1:29, " behold the Lamb of God who takes away the sin of the world."] As a prophet, John said, " Lamb of God "; as more than a prophet [Matt. 11:9] he said, " who takes away the sin of the world." The first expression concerns his [Christ's] body; the second, him who was in the body. As the lamb is imperfect in the genus of sheep, so the body is imperfect by comparison with him who dwells in it. If he had wanted to ascribe perfection to the body, he would have spoken of a ram which was to be sacrificed.

11. [John 2:12, " after this he descended to Capernaum."] This again means the beginning of another dispensation, since

" he descended " was not spoken idly. Capernaum means on
the one hand the ends of the world, on the other the material
things to which he descended. And because the place was alien
to him, nothing is reported as having been done or said in it.

12. [John 2: 13, " and the Passover of the Jews was near."]
The great feast itself; for it was a symbol of the passion of the
Saviour, when the sheep not only was slain but when eaten
provided rest. When sacrificed it signified the passion of the
Saviour in the world; when eaten it signified the rest which
is in marriage.

13. [John 2: 13-15, " and Jesus ascended to Jerusalem,
and he found in the temple those who sold oxen . . . and
he made a whip of small cords."] The ascent to Jerusalem signifies the ascent of the Lord from material things to
the psychic place, which is an image of Jerusalem. He
found them in the holy place [*hieron*], not in the temple as a
whole [*naos*], so that it might not be supposed that simple
" calling," apart from the Spirit, is assisted by the Lord; for
the holy place is the Holy of Holies, into which only the High
Priest enters [Heb. 9: 7], where the spirituals come. But the
court of the temple, where the Levites also are, is a symbol of
the psychics outside the Pleroma who are found to be in
salvation. Those who are found in the holy place selling oxen
and sheep and doves, and the money changers sitting there, are
those who give nothing freely but regard the coming of strangers
to the temple as an occasion for trade and gain, and because
of their own profit and love of money supply the sacrifices for
the worship of God. The whip which Jesus made of small
cords is an image of the power and energy of the Holy Spirit,
blowing out the wicked. The whip and the linen [Rev. 15: 6]
and the winding-sheet [Matt. 27: 59] and other things of this
kind are an image of the power and energy of the Holy Spirit.
The whip was tied on wood, and this wood was a symbol of
the cross. On this wood were nailed up and destroyed the
gambling merchants and all wickedness [cf. Col. 2: 14]. Of
these two substances the whip was made; for Jesus did not
make it of dead leather, for he desired to construct the church

as no longer a den of thieves and merchants but as a house of his Father.

14. [John 2: 17, " the zeal of thy house shall consume me."] Spoken in the role of those powers which were cast out and consumed by the Saviour.

15. [John 2: 19, " in three days I will raise it up."] " In three days " rather than " on the third," which is the spiritual day of the resurrection of the church. [Consequently, says Origen, the first is earthly and the second is psychic.]

16. [John 2: 20, " this temple has been building for forty-six years."] Solomon's building the temple of forty-six years is an image of the Saviour, and the number six refers to matter, i.e., that which is formed, while forty, which is the uncombined Tetrad, to the inbreathing [Gen. 2: 7] and the seed in the inbreathing.

17. [John 4: 12ff.; the Samaritan woman at Jacob's well.] That well signified insipid, temporary, and deficient life and its glory; for it was worldly. This is proved by the fact that Jacob's cattle drank from it. But the water which the Saviour gave is of his Spirit and Power. " You will never thirst," for his life is eternal and will never perish like the first [water] from the well, but is permanent. For the grace and the gift of our Saviour are not to be taken away or consumed or corrupted by the one who shares in them. The first life [however] is perishable. " Water springing up to eternal life " refers to those who receive the life supplied richly from above and themselves pour forth what has been supplied them for the eternal life of others. The Samaritan woman exhibited uncritical faith, alien to her nature, when she did not hesitate over what he was saying to her. " Give me this water ": she hated the shallows pierced by the word, as well as that place of so-called living water. The woman says these things to show forth the toilsome and laborious and unnourishing quality of that water.

18. [John 4: 16ff.; the Samaritan woman and her previous husbands.] It is obvious that this means [" If you wish to receive this water, go, call your husband "] the Pleroma of the

Samaritan woman, so that coming with him to the Saviour she might receive from him power and union and mixture with her Pleroma. He was speaking to her about an earthly husband, to call him, since he knew that she did not have a lawful husband. The Saviour said to her, " Call your husband and come here," meaning her fellow [*syzygos*] from the Pleroma. As for what was meant [allegorically] she was ignorant of her own husband; as for the simple sense, she was ashamed to say that she had an adulterer, not a husband. " Truly you said you had no husband," since in the world the Samaritan woman had no husband, for her husband was in the Aeon. The " six husbands " signify all the material evil to which she was bound and with which she consorted when she was irrationally debauched, insulted, rejected, and abandoned by them.

19. [John 4: 19ff.; the Samaritan woman and Samaritan worship.] The Samaritan woman properly acknowledged what was said by him to her; for it is characteristic only of a prophet to know all things. She acted as suited her nature, neither lying nor explicitly acknowledging her immorality. Persuaded that he was a prophet, she asked him and at the same time revealed the cause of her fornication, because on account of ignorance of God she had neglected the worship of God and everything necessary for her life, and was otherwise [. . .] in life; for she would not have come to the well which was outside the city [unless she had] wanted to learn in what way, and pleasing whom, and worshipping God, she might escape from fornication; therefore she said, " Our fathers worshipped on this mountain," etc.

20. [John 4: 21, " believe me, woman . . . neither on this mountain nor in Jerusalem will you worship the Father."] Earlier Jesus did not say, " Believe me, woman "; now he thus commands her. The mountain means the devil or his world, since the devil was one part of the whole of matter, and the whole world is a mountain of evil, a deserted dwelling of beasts, which all [Jews] prior to the law and all the Gentiles worship; Jerusalem is the creation or the Creator, whom the

Jews worship. In a second sense the mountain is the creation, which the Gentiles worship, and Jerusalem is the Creator, whom the Jews worship. So you, as the spirituals, will worship neither the creation nor the Demiurge, but the Father of Truth. And he accepts her as one already faithful and to be numbered with the worshippers in truth.

21. [John 4: 22, " you worship what you do not know."] These are the Jews and the Gentiles. As Peter [*Kerygma Petri*] teaches, " We must not worship in Greek fashion, accepting the works of matter and worshipping wood and stone, or in Jewish fashion worship the divine; for they, thinking that they alone know God, do not know him, and worship angels and the month and the moon." *

22. [John 4: 22, " we worship what we know, for salvation is of the Jews."] " We " means the one who is in the Aeon and those who have come with him; for these knew the one they worship, worshipping in truth. " Salvation is from the Jews " because it was in Judaea, but not in them [" for he was not pleased with all of them," 1 Cor. 10: 5], and because from that race came salvation and the Logos to the world. In terms of what was meant [allegorically] salvation came from the Jews, since they are regarded as images of beings in the Pleroma. Previous worshippers worshipped him who was not father, in flesh and error. They worshipped the creation, not the true Creator, who is Christ, since " All things came into being through him, and outside him nothing came into being."

23. [John 4: 23, " the Father seeks such to worship him."] In the deep matter of error has been lost that which is related to the Father; this is sought for so that the Father may be worshipped by his kin.

24. [John 4: 24, " God is Spirit, and those who worship must worship in spirit and in truth."] Undefiled and pure and invisible is his divine nature; and worthily of him who is worshipped [one must worship] in spiritual, not fleshly fashion.

* This passage from the apocryphal *Kerygma* is quoted more fully by Clement of Alexandria (*Strom.* iv. 39-41).

For those who are of the same nature as the Father are spirit, those who worship in truth and not in error, as the Apostle teaches when he calls this worship " spiritual [rational] service " [Rom. 12: 1].

25. [John 4: 25, " I know that Messiah comes, who is called Christ."] The church expected Christ and believed of him that he alone would know all things.

26. [John 4: 26, " I who speak to you am he."] Since the Samaritan woman was convinced that when Christ came he would proclaim everything to her, he said, " Know that I who speak to you am he whom you expected." And when he acknowledged himself as the expected one who had come, " his disciples came to him," for on their account he had come to Samaria.

27. [John 4: 28, " the woman left her water-jug."] The water-jug which can receive life is the condition and thought of the power which is with the Saviour. She left it with him, that is, she had such a vessel with the Saviour, a vessel in which she had come to get living water, and she returned to the world, proclaiming the coming of Christ to the " calling." For through the Spirit and by the Spirit the soul is brought to the Saviour. " They went out of the city," i.e., out of their former worldly way of life; and through faith they came to the Saviour.

28. [John 4: 31, " the disciples said, ' Rabbi, eat.' "] They wanted to share with him some of what they had obtained by buying it from Samaria.

29. [John 4: 32, " I have food to eat that you do not know."] Heracleon said nothing on the text.

30. [John 4: 33, " Did anyone bring anything for him to eat? "] The disciples understood in a low way and imitated the Samaritan woman, who said, " You have no dipper, and the well is deep."

31. [John 4: 34, " My meat is to do the will of him who sent me."] The Saviour thus narrated to the disciples that this was the subject of his discussion with the woman, calling the will of the Father his " meat "; for this was his food and

rest and power. The will of the Father is for men to know the Father and be saved; this was the work of the Saviour, on account of which he was sent into Samaria, i.e., into the world.

32. [John 4: 35, " the harvest comes."] He speaks of the harvest of the fruits as if it had a fixed interval of four months, and yet the harvest of which he was speaking was already present. The harvest is that of the souls of believers. They are already ripe and ready for harvest and suitable for gathering into the barn [cf. Matt. 13: 30], i.e., through faith into rest, as many as are ready. For not all are ready; some are already ready, others are going to be; others are already oversown [cf. Matt. 13: 25].

33. [Matt. 9: 37, " the harvest is great, but the labourers are few."] This refers to those who are ready for harvest and suitable for gathering already into the barn through faith into rest, and suited for salvation and reception of the Logos.

34. [John 4: 36, " he who reaps receives a wage."] This is said since the Saviour calls himself a reaper. And the wage of our Lord is the salvation and restoration of those reaped, i.e. his rest upon them. " And he gathers fruit for eternal life " means either that what is gathered is the fruit of eternal life or that it itself is eternal life.

35. [John 4: 37, " so that the sower may rejoice together with the reaper."] For the sower rejoices because he sows, and because he already gathers some of his seeds; similarly the reaper, because he reaps. But the first one began by sowing and the second one, by reaping. They could not both begin with the same thing, since sowing is first, then afterwards reaping. When the sower stops sowing, the reaper still reaps; but at the present time both effect their own works but rejoice in a common joy when they consider the perfection of the seeds. " One sows and another reaps." The Son of Man above the Place sows [cf. Matt. 13: 37]; the Saviour, who is himself also Son of Man, reaps and sends as reapers the angels known through the disciples [Matt. 13: 39], each for his own soul.

36. [John 4: 38, " others laboured, and you have entered into their labour."] These seeds were sown neither through them nor by them; those who laboured are the angels of the dispensation, through whom, as mediators [cf. Gal. 3: 19], they were sown and nourished. The labour of sowers and reapers is not the same, for the former, in cold and wet and toil dig up the earth and sow, and throughout the winter look after it, hoeing it and pulling out weeds; but the latter, entering upon a prepared fruit, reap harvests with gladness.

37. [John 4: 39, " out of that city many believed because of the woman's report."] Out of that city, i.e., out of the world. Through the woman's report, i.e., through the spiritual church. Many, since there are many psychics, but the imperishable nature of the election is one and uniform and unique.

38. [John 4: 40, " he remained there two days."] He remained " with them " and not " in them," and for two days, either [to signify] the present Aeon and the future one in marriage, or the time before his passion and that after the passion, which he spent with them, and when after converting many more to faith through his own word he departed from them.

39. [John 4: 42, " we no longer believe because of your word."] It ought to say, " only your word." " For we ourselves have heard and know that this is the Saviour of the world." At first men are led by others to belief in the Saviour, but when they read his words, they no longer believe because of human testimony alone, but because of the truth itself.

40. [John 4: 46ff.; the royal officer's son and his healing.] The royal officer is the Demiurge, since he himself reigned over those under him; but because his dominion is small and temporary he was called a " royal officer," like some petty king set over a small kingdom by a universal king. His son, in Capernaum, is in the lower part of the intermediate area* by the sea, i.e., in that which adjoins matter. In other words, the man belonging to him was sick, i.e., not in accordance with nature but in ignorance and sins. " From Judaea to Galilee "

---

* The place of the Middle, as in Hippolytus, *Ref.* 6, 32, 7 (Brooke).

[4: 47] means " from the Judaea above." The expression " he was about to die " refutes the doctrines of those who suppose that the soul is immortal; soul and body are destroyed in Gehenna [Matt. 10: 28]. The soul is not immortal but only has a disposition towards salvation; it is the perishable which puts on imperishability and the mortal which puts on immortality, when its death was swallowed in victory [1 Cor. 15: 53-55]. " Unless you see signs and wonders you will not believe " [4: 48] was properly spoken to such a person as had the nature to be persuaded through works and through sense-perception, not to believe a word. " Descend before my child dies," because the end of the law was death [cf. Rom. 7: 13]; the law kills through sins. So before death was finally effected in accordance with sins, the father asks the only Saviour to help the son, i.e., a nature of this kind. " Your son lives " [4: 40] the Saviour said in modesty, since he did not say, " Let him live," or show that he himself had provided life. Having descended to the sick man and healing him of the disease, i.e., of sins, and having made him alive through remission, he said, " Your son lives." " The man believed " because the Demiurge can easily believe that the Saviour is able to heal even when not present. The slaves of the royal officer [4: 51] are the angels of the Demiurge, proclaiming, " Your child lives," because he is behaving properly and rightly, no longer doing what is unsuitable. For this reason the slaves proclaimed to the royal officer the news about his son's salvation, because the angels are the first to observe the actions of men on earth to see if they have lived well and sincerely since the Saviour's sojourn. " The seventh hour " refers to the nature of the man healed. " He and his whole house believed " [4: 53] refers to the angelic order and men related to him. It is a question whether some angels will be saved, those who descended upon the daughters of men [Gen. 6: 2]. The destruction of the men of the Demiurge is made plain by " The sons of the kingdom will go out into the outer darkness " [Matt. 8: 12]. Concerning them Isaiah prophesied [1: 2, 4; 5: 1], " I begot and raised up sons, but they set me aside;"

he calls them " alien sons and a wicked and lawless seed and a vineyard producing thorns."

41. [John 8:21, " where I go you cannot come."] How can they come to be in imperishability when they are in ignorance and disbelief and sins?

42. [John 8:22, " will he kill himself? "] In their wicked thoughts the Jews said these things and declared themselves greater than the Saviour and supposed that they would go away to God for eternal rest, but the Saviour would slay himself and go to corruption and death, where they did not think they would go. The Jews thought the Saviour said, " When I have slain myself I shall go to corruption, where you cannot come."

43. [John 8:37, " my word does not abide in you."] It does not abide because they are unsuited for it either by substance or by inclination.

44. [John 8:44, " you are of your father, the devil."] This gives the reason for their inability to hear the word of Jesus or to understand his speech. It means " of the substance of the devil." This makes their nature evident to them, and convicts them in advance, for they are neither children of Abraham [for they would not have hated Jesus] nor children of God, because they do not love him [Jesus].

45. [John 8:44]. Those to whom the word was spoken were of the substance of the devil.

46. [John 8:44, " you wish to perform the desires of your father."] The devil has not will but desires. These things were spoken not to those by nature sons of the devil, the men of earth, but to the psychics, who are sons of the devil by adoption: some of them who are such by nature can become sons of God by adoption. From having loved the desires of the devil and performing them, these men become children of the devil, though they are not such by nature. The name " children " must be understood in three ways; first by nature, second by inclination, third by merit. By nature means that which is generated by some generator, which is properly called " child "; by inclination, when one does

someone's will by his own inclination and is called the child
of him whose will he does; by merit, in the way that some are
called children of Gehenna and of darkness and of lawlessness
[cf. Matt. 23: 15, 33], and offspring of snakes and vipers [Matt.
3: 7], for these [parents] do not generate anything by nature
their own; they are ruinous and consume those who are cast
into them. But since they do their works, they are called their
children. He [Jesus] calls them children of the devil, not
because the devil generates offspring, but because by doing
the works of the devil they became like him.

47. [John 8: 44.] For his nature is not of the truth, but of
the opposite to the truth, of error and ignorance. Therefore
he can neither stand in truth nor have truth in himself; he
has falsehood as his own by his own nature, being by nature
unable ever to speak truth. Not only is he a liar, but so is his
father, i.e., his nature, since he originated from error and
falsity.

48. [John 8: 50, " there is one who seeks and judges."]
The one who seeks and judges is the one who avenges me, the
servant commissioned for this, the one who bears not the
sword in vain [Rom. 13: 4], the king's avenger; and this is
Moses, in accordance with what he previously said to them,
" On whom you have set your hope " [John 5: 45]. The judge
and punisher is Moses, i.e., the legislator himself. How then
does he say that all judgment has been delivered to him?
[cf. John 5: 27]. He speaks rightly, for the judge who does
his will judges as a servant, as appears to be the case among
men.

[This is the last fragment preserved by Origen in his
Commentary on John; the two remaining ones come from
Origen's predecessor, Clement of Alexandria.]

49. [Matt. 3: 11.] John said, " I baptize you with water,
but after me comes one who baptizes you in spirit and fire."
He baptized no one with fire; but some understand by " fire "
the ears of those who are sealed (in baptism) and thus have
heard the apostolic [preaching]. [*Eclogae propheticae* xxv. 1].

50. [Matt. 10: 32-33, " whoever confesses [in] me before

men . . . ."] One kind of confession is made by faith and conduct, another by voice. The confession by voice also takes place before the authorities; the multitude considers this the only confession—wrongly, for hypocrites too can make this confession. This word will not be found expressed universally, for not all those who are saved made the confession by voice and departed. Among these [exceptions] are Matthew, Philip, Thomas, Levi, and many others. The confession by voice is not universal but particular. But that which he here mentions is universal, the one by works and actions corresponding to faith in him. This confession is followed by the particular one before the authorities, if it is necessary and reason requires it. For this man will confess by voice as well, if he has previously rightly confessed by [his] disposition.

And he correctly said " in me " of those who confess, and " me " of those who deny. For the latter deny him, even if they confess him by voice, when they do not confess by action. The only ones who confess " in him " are those who live in confession and action related to him; he confesses " in them " since he is wrapped up in them and held by them. Therefore they can never deny him; but those who are not in him deny him. For he did not say, " Whoever will deny *in* me," but " me." For no one who is in him ever denies him. " Before men," both the saved and the Gentiles in similar fashion, by conduct also before the former and by voice also before the latter [*Strom.* iv. 71-72].

[Fragment 51 is merely a remark by Photius.]

PART VI

SELECTIONS FROM THE
HERMETIC WRITINGS

The Hermetic writings, so called because in many of them there is a revealer called Hermes (sometimes identified with the Egyptian god Thoth or Tat), are semi-gnostic or "gnosticising" treatises probably written between the second century of our era and the fourth. Preserved as well as written, in Greek, they present several different kinds of popular religious philosophy in the dress of revelation. Some of them have been found in the Nag-Hammadi collection of books read by Gnostics.

On the Hermetica see R. Reitzenstein, ' Poimandres ' (Leipzig, 1904); J. Kroll, ' Die Lehren des Hermes Trismegistos ' (Münster, 1914, reprinted 1928); W. Scott—A. S. Ferguson, ' Hermetica,' I-IV (Oxford, 1924-1936); C. H. Dodd, ' The Bible and the Greeks ' (London, 1935); A.-J. Festugiere, ' La révélation d'Hermès Trismégiste,' I-IV (Paris, 1944-1954); M. P. Nilsson, ' Geschichte der griechischen Religion,' II (Munich, 1950), 556-96; H. Gundel, " Poimandres," Pauly-Wissowa, ' Realencyclopädie der classischen Altertumswissenschaft,' XXI, 1193-1207); G. van Moorsel, 'The Mysteries of Hermes Trismegistus' (Utrecht, 1955).

The only reliable text of the Hermetica is that of A. D. Nock—A.-J. Festugiere, ' Hermès Trismégiste,' I-IV (Paris, 1945-1954).

Tractate I (Poimandres)

The first treatise is known as Poimandres because of the name given the revealer in it. It probably dates from the second century of our era; a late third-century Greek papyrus (P. Berol. 9794) combines chapters 31 and 32 with a Christian doxology. In it we find a mixture of popular philosophy and theosophy with the creation story of the book of Genesis. Cf. E. Haenchen, " Aufbau und Theologie des ' Poimandres,' " ' Zeitschrift für Theologie und Kirche ' 53 (1956), 149-91.

(1) One day, when I had begun to reflect upon the things that truly exist and my thoughts had soared aloft, while my bodily senses were bridled like those borne down by sleep through surfeit of food or fatigue of the body, it seemed to me that a being of vast, immeasurable size drew near and called me by name and said, " What do you wish to hear and see and by thinking come to learn and know? " (2) I replied, " Who are you? " And he said, " I am Poimandres, the Mind of the Absolute Sovereignty [*authentia*]. I know what you want, and I am with you everywhere." (3) I said, " I desire to learn the things that really exist and to understand their nature and to know God. How I desire to hear! " And he replied to me, " Keep in your mind the things you desire to learn, and I will teach you."

(4) At these words he changed his form, and instantly everything opened up to me, and I saw a limitless vision, everything having become a light, serene and happy, and I

was enraptured by the sight. After a little a darkness, produced bit by bit, came bearing down, and it was terrifying
and abhorrent, coiling itself in spirals like a serpent, as it
seemed. Then this darkness was changed into a kind of moist
nature, indescribably shaken, and exuding smoke as from a
fire, and emitting a kind of voice, an unutterable groaning.
Then from it came an inarticulate cry, which it sent forth,
like a voice of fire, (5) and from the light [. . .] A holy Logos
came upon Nature, and an unmixed fire leaped forth from
the moist nature upwards towards the height. It was light and
swift and active, and the air, being light, followed the [fiery]
spirit, rising up from earth and water to the fire, so that it
seemed to be suspended from the fire. The earth and the water
remained where they were, mingled together so that the earth
could not be seen apart from the water. But it was moved
in obedience to the spiritual Logos which was " borne over
it " [Gen. 1 : 2].

(6) Then Poimandres said to me, " Do you understand
what this vision means? " " I should like to know," I replied.
" That light," he said, " is I, Mind, your God, who existed
before the moist nature which appeared out of the darkness.
And the luminous Logos which came out of Mind is the Son
of God." " How so ? " I asked. " Understand it this way,"
he replied. " That which in you sees and hears is the Logos
of the Lord, and your Mind is God the Father. The two are
not separated from each other; life consists in their union."
" I thank you," I said. " But think about the light," he said,
" and understand this."

(7) When he had said this he gazed at me a long time, so
that I trembled at his appearance. Then, when he had
raised his head, I beheld in my Mind the light consisting of
innumerable powers which had now become a boundless
ordered cosmos, though the fire was surrounded by a mighty
force, and being firmly held was kept stable. This is what I was
thinking of as I looked at it, encouraged by what Poimandres
told me. (8) While I was thus struck with amazement, he
spoke to me again: " You see by Mind the archetypal form,

the primal principle, prior to the limitless beginning." That is what Poimandres said to me. I said, "What about the elements of nature—whence did they arise?" And again he replied to this, "From the Will of God, which, having received the Logos, and beholding the beautiful cosmos, imitated it, since it [the Will] was fashioned as an ordered world by its own proper elements and products, i.e., souls.

(9) "But Mind, which is God, being both male and female, and existing as life and light, begot by a word [Logos] another Mind, the Demiurge; and he, being God of fire and of spirit, created certain governors, seven in number, to surround the sensible world with their circles. Their governing is called Destiny. (10) At once the Logos of God leaped out of the downward-moving elements into the pure region of Nature, just created, and united itself with the Demiurge Mind, for it was of the same nature as it, and thus the lower elements of nature were left to themselves, deprived of reason [*logos*], and so became nothing more than mere matter. (11) But the Demiurge Mind, joined with the Logos, surrounding the circles and compelling them to turn as they rush along, thus set his creatures revolving, and let them turn about from an invisible point of departure to an unfixed goal; for their revolution begins where it ends. And the rotation of these, as Mind willed it, produces, from the downward-bearing elements, creatures without reason [for they retain no share of the Logos], while the air produces things that fly and the water, things that swim. Earth and water are [now] separated from each other, in accordance with the Will of Mind [cf. Gen. 1:9], and the earth brought forth from itself the animals that were in it, quadrupeds and reptiles, wild beasts and tame [cf. Gen. 1:24].

(12) "But Mind, the Father of all, being life and light, gave birth to a Man like himself; with him he was pleased, as his own offspring, for the Man was very beautiful, bearing the image of his Father. For truly God was pleased with his own form, and he delivered all his creatures to him [cf. Gen. 1:26-28]. (13) Having observed the creation made by the

Demiurge in the fire, Man himself desired to create, and permission was granted by the Father. So entering the creative
sphere, where he received all power, he observed the things
created by his brother; and the Governors were pleased with
him, and each gave him a share in his own region.

" Then having learned their substance and having received
a share in their nature, he desired to break out of the bounds
of their orbits, and to know the power of him who reigns over
the fire. (14) So Man, who possessed all authority over the
world of mortal things and of irrational animals, bent down
through the composite framework of the spheres, having torn
off the covering, and showed to downward-tending Nature
the beautiful form of God. When Nature beheld the never-
satiating beauty of the one who possesses in himself all the
energy of the Governors, and likewise the form of God, she
smiled with love, for she had seen the image of Man's wonder-
fully beautiful form reflected in the water, and his shadow
on the earth. And he, having seen in her this form like himself, reflected in the water, loved it and desired to live in it.
With the will came the action, and thus he came to occupy a
form devoid of reason. Nature, having received the form she
loved, folded him to herself, and so they were united; for they
passionately loved each other.

(15) " For this reason man, unlike all other creatures on
earth, is dual in nature, mortal because of the body and
immortal because of the essential Man. For being immortal
and having authority over all things, he suffers the condition
of mortals since he is subject to Destiny. Though he is superior
to the framework, he has become a slave in it. And although
created male and female because of his derivation from the
bisexual Father, and sleepless from the unsleeping one, he is
nevertheless overcome by [love and sleep?]."

(16) And after this [. . .] " O my Mind, for I too love the
teaching." And Poimandres said, " This is the mystery which
has been hidden until this very day. Nature, mingling in
intercourse with Man, brought forth a marvel most marvellous. Since Man had in himself the nature of the framework

of the Seven, which as I told you are composed of fire and spirit, Nature did not delay, but at once gave birth to seven men corresponding to the natures of the seven Governors, bisexual and sublime." After this I said, " O Poimandres, now I have reached the utmost point of desire and longing to hear. Do not leave the subject!" And Poimandres replied, " Then keep still—I have not yet finished the first point." " See, I am still," I said.

(17) " So it came to pass, as I was saying, that the birth of these seven took place in the following way. Earth was female, and water the generative element; by the fire they were developed. From the ether Nature took the spirit, and produced their bodies after the likeness of the Man. But the Man, being formed of life and light, changed himself into soul and mind, forming soul out of life and mind out of light. And so all things in the sensible world continued until the end of a period and the beginnings of species.

(18) " Now hear the teaching you have been longing to hear. When this period was fulfilled, the bond uniting all things was broken by the will of God. For all living creatures, previously bisexual, were parted, as was man; they became on the one hand male, on the other, female. At once God spoke by a holy word [*Logos*], ' Increase and multiply, all creatures and creations [cf. Gen. 1: 28], and let him who has a mind recognise himself as immortal, and know that the cause of death is love, and know all the things that exist.'

(19) " When God had spoken thus, Providence, by means of Destiny and the framework of the spheres, brought about unions and set births in process, and all things were multiplied after their kind [cf. Gen. 1: 12]. He who has recognised himself has come into that good which is best of all; but he who has loved the body, which comes from the deceit of love, remains wandering in the darkness, suffering in his senses the things of death."

(20) " But what great sin," I asked, " have they committed, who are thus ignorant, so that they were deprived of immortality?" " You seem to me, indeed," he said, " not to have

reflected on what you have heard. Did I not tell you to think?"
" I am thinking," I replied, " and I remember, and I am grateful to you for it." " If you understand," he said to me, " tell
me why those who are in death deserve to die." I replied,
" It is because the source of the individual body is that
abhorrent darkness, from which the moist nature comes, and
from which the body is produced in the sensible world, and
by which death is nourished." (21) " You have understood
correctly, O man," he replied; " but how is it that ' he who
understands himself departs from himself,' as the word of
God says?" I said, " It is because the Father of the All consists of light and life, and from him is begotten the Man."
" You have spoken well," he replied. " Light and life, this is
God the Father, from whom the Man is begotten. If then
you learn that he is light and life, and that you too are formed
from these, you will depart again into life." This is what
Poimandres said.

" But tell me something more," I said. " How shall I
depart into life, O my Mind? For God said, ' Let the man
who has Mind recognise himself.' (22) Do not all men possess
Mind?" " Watch your words, my friend!" he replied. " I
myself, Mind, dwell with the holy and good, the pure and
merciful, the pious; and my presence is a help to them, and
at once they know all things and they worship the Father in
love. And they give thanks, blessing and singing hymns in
orderly fashion, with filial devotion. And before abandoning
the body to its proper death, they despise the senses, since
they know what the activities of the senses are. Nay, even
more, I myself, Mind, will not permit the assailing activities
of the body to take effect. I am the guardian of the gates and
I lock the door against the entry of evil and shameful actions,
cutting off their imaginations. (23) But I am far removed
from foolish, evil, wicked, envious, covetous, murderous, and
godless men. I yield place to the avenging demon, and he
applies to such a man the sharpness of fire, piercing his senses
[?] and arming him for still worse deeds of lawlessness so that
he shall receive even harsher punishment. So the man does

not cease having a desire for his limitless appetites, insatiably fighting in the dark, and this torments him and increases the fire upon him."

(24) "You have taught me well, O Mind, all that I desired. Tell me just one thing more, about the ascent which takes place." To this Poimandres replied, "First, in the dissolution of the material body, you deliver the body itself to be changed, and the form you possessed vanishes, and you deliver to the demon your character which is henceforth to be inactive, while the senses of the body return to their sources, of which they become part, and are once more identified with the Powers; but anger and lust depart to the irrational nature. (25) And so man henceforth presses upwards through the composite framework. In the first zone he yields up the power to increase and decrease; in the second, the power to contrive evil, a deceit [henceforth] ineffective; in the third, deceitful lust, [henceforth] ineffective; in the fourth, arrogant ostentation, [now] deprived of its intended effects; in the fifth, unholy audacity and rash boldness; in the sixth, the lawless appetite given by wealth, [henceforth] ineffective; and in the seventh, the lie that sets a snare. (26) Then, stripped bare of all that the powers in the framework had wrought in it, man enters the eighth [*ogdoadic*] nature, possessing only his own proper power, and, together with the beings which are found there, he hymns the Father. Those who are present rejoice over his arrival; and being made like those with whom he dwells, he also hears a kind of sweet sound of certain Powers, who dwell above the eighth nature, as they praise God. Then, moving in proper order, they mount up to the Father, and yield themselves to the Powers, and having themselves become Powers they enter into God. Such is the blissful goal of those who possess knowledge [*gnosis*]—to become God. Why then do you delay? Now that you have received all things from me, should you not become a guide to those who are worthy, so that through you the race of mankind may be saved by God?"

(27) Having said this to me, Poimandres mingled with the Powers. And after I had rendered thanks and had blessed the

Father of the All, I was sent forth by him, having been empowered and fully taught about the nature of the All and the supreme vision. And I began to preach to men the beauty of piety and of knowledge [*gnosis*]: " O ye peoples, men born of earth, you who have given yourselves up to drunkenness and slumber and ignorance of God, be sober, cease your debauchery, enchanted with the sorcery of irrational sleep! " (28) And as they heard this, they gathered about me with one accord. And I said, " Men born of earth, why have you given yourselves over to death, when you have the power to partake of immortality? Repent, you who have journeyed with error and kept company with ignorance! Free yourselves from the shadowy light, lay hold on immortality, forsaking corruption! "

(29) And some of them mocked me and stood apart, for they had given themselves over to the way of death; others threw themselves at my feet and begged for instruction. I raised them up and became the guide of mankind, teaching the doctrine of how and in what manner they should be saved. And I sowed in them the words of wisdom, and they were nourished with the ambrosial water. And when evening came and the sun's rays were beginning to decline completely, I bade them give thanks to God. When they had completed the thanksgiving, each of them betook himself to his own bed.

(30) But I wrote down for myself the benefaction of Poimandres, and being filled with what I had wanted I greatly rejoiced. For the sleep of the body became wakefulness of the soul, and the closing of the eyes true vision, and my silence gestation with the good, and the utterance of the word a birth of good things. And all this came to pass for me when I received [it] from my Mind, i.e., from Poimandres, the Logos of the Absolute Sovereignty. And so, being divinely inspired by the truth, I have come. Therefore with all my soul and strength I give praise to God the Father.

(31) " Holy is God, the Father of the All.

      " Holy is God, whose Will is accomplished by his own
          Powers.

" Holy is God, who wills to be known and is known by
his own.

" Holy art thou, who by Logos has constituted all
existing things.

" Holy art thou, of whom all Nature was born as the
image.

" Holy art thou, whom Nature has not formed.

" Holy art thou, who art more mighty than all Power.

" Holy art thou, who art greater than all eminence.

" Holy art thou, who art superior to all praises.

" Accept the pure spiritual sacrifices from a soul and heart
uplifted to thee, O inexpressible, ineffable one, named only by
silence! (32) Grant me this prayer, and fill me with power,
who implore thee that I may never fall away from the knowledge [*gnosis*] which is fit for our nature; that with this grace
I may illuminate those of our race who are in ignorance, my
brethren, thy sons. Yea, I believe, and bear witness. I enter
into life and light. Blessed art thou, O Father; thy Man longs
to share with thee in the work of sanctification, even as thou
hast given all authority unto him [cf. John 17: 2, 19]."

Tractate IV (*The Krater or the Monad*)

A DISCOURSE OF HERMES TO TAT

(1) Since the Demiurge created the whole cosmos, not by the use of hands but by word, he conceived it as present and ever-existing and as having produced all things [i.e., perfect?] and the One-Only, having by his own will created the things that are. For this is the body of that One, intangible, invisible, immeasurable, inextensible; nor is it like to any other body. It is not fire, nor water, nor air, nor breath; but all things are from [i.e., have been made by] him. For since he is good, he did not will to set up this [universe] as an offering to himself alone, and to adorn the earth, but (2) he sent down man as an ornament of the divine body, a mortal creature adorning an immortal. And the cosmos of living creatures undertook to seize the ever-living, while man [laid hold upon] both the word and the mind of the cosmos. For man became the witness of the work of God, and marvelled, and came to know its Maker.

(3) Now speech, O Tat, he imparted to all men; but mind he did not impart to all. Not that he grudged it to any; for the grudging temper does not come from above, but is produced here below, in the souls of men who do not possess mind. [Tat:] Why then, Father, did not God impart mind

to all men? [Hermes:] It was his will, my son, that [mind] should be set up in the midst as a prize for human souls [to win]. (4) [Tat:] And where did he place it? [Hermes:] He filled a great crater with it [i.e., with mind], and sent it down; and he appointed a herald, and bade him proclaim to the hearts of men as follows: "O heart, baptize yourself in this crater, if you are able, believing that you shall ascend to the One who sent down the crater, and recognising for what purpose you have been made."

As many therefore as paid attention to the proclamation, and baptized themselves in the mind, partook of knowledge [*gnosis*], and became perfect [or complete] men [*teleioi*], having received mind. But those who failed to heed the proclamation, these are the ones who possess speech [*hoi logikoi*], but have not in addition received mind, not knowing the purpose for which they were created, nor by whom [*plural*]. (5) The sensations of these men closely resemble those of irrational animals, and are a mixture of anger and passion; they do not admire the things that are worthy of contemplation, and they pay attention only to the pleasures and appetites of the body, and believe that man has been born for the sake of such things. But on the other hand, as many as partook of the gift sent by God, these, O Tat, when you compare their works, are as immortal gods to mortal men, embracing all things in their own mind, the things on earth and the things in heaven, and even whatever may be above heaven. Having thus raised themselves to such a height, they see the Good, and having seen it they look upon their sojourn here below as a misfortune. Then, having scorned all things corporeal and incorporeal, they hasten on to the One and Only. (6) This, O Tat, is the knowledge of the mind, the open way to things divine, and the comprehension of God, for the Crater is divine.

[Tat:] I too would be baptized, O Father. [Hermes:] If you do not first hate your body, my son, you cannot love yourself. But if you love yourself, you will possess mind; and possessing mind, you will partake of knowledge also. [Tat:]

What do you mean, Father? [Hermes:] It is impossible, my son, to concern yourself with both [at once], with things mortal and with things divine. For since there are two kinds of things, the corporeal and the incorporeal, and since that which is mortal is of one kind and that which is divine is of the other, a choice of one or the other is left open to the one who wishes to choose [it]. It is not possible to choose both; . . . and when one is rejected, this shows the force of the other. (7) The choice of the better is not only a credit to the one who has made the choice, since it deifies the man, but it also manifests piety towards God. But the choice of the worse destroys the man, and is no less offensive to God; at the very least, like processions that pass along a middle way, but can do nothing themselves and only obstruct the way for others, so these men merely pass in procession in the cosmos, led along by bodily pleasures.

(8) This being the case, O Tat, the things that come from God are always at hand, and always will be; and the part that belongs to us—let it follow, and not fall short! For God is not to blame; it is we who are to blame for our evils, since we prefer them to the good. You see, my son, through how many bodies [i.e., physical spheres] we must make our way, and through how many choirs of daemons and series and courses of stars, in order to press on towards the One and Only [God]. For one can never cross over to the farther boundary of the Good; it is limitless, and without end; in itself, it is without beginning, though for us it seems to have a beginning when we [first] gain knowledge of it. (9) But the knowledge of it is not the beginning of the thing itself; it is only the beginning of its being known. Let us lay hold, then, upon this beginning, and let us go forward with all speed; for it is very hard for us to forsake the familiar things that surround us and turn back to things ancient and aboriginal. The things that are seen delight us, while the things that are unseen lead us to doubt. But the things that are evil are the most visible, while the Good is invisible to things that are seen, since it has no form nor figure. For this reason it is like

itself, and unlike all others: it is impossible for the incorporeal to be manifested to the corporeal. (10) This is the difference between the like and the unlike, and the defect of the unlike in relation to the like.

. . . For the Monad, being the beginning [i.e., source] and root of all things, is in all things, as if it were the root and beginning. Apart from a beginning nothing exists; but the beginning is not derived from anything, but springs from itself, if it is indeed the source of all other things. The Monad, therefore, being the beginning [arche] embraces in itself every number, and is embraced by none of them; it generates every number, and is generated by no other. (11) Now everything that is generated is imperfect and divisible, and may be increased or decreased; but none of this happens to what is perfect. And if that which may be increased derives its increase from the monad, it also suffers from its own weakness when it is incapable of retaining the one.

And so, Tat, as far as it is possible you have had drawn for you an image of God; and if you look carefully [at it], and study it with the eyes of your heart, believe me, my son, you will find the path that leads upwards; or rather, the image itself will lead you along. For the sight of it has its own peculiar power; it takes hold of those who have once caught sight of it and draws them upwards, just as they say the magnet attracts iron.

3

Tractate VII (Ignorance of God)

THAT IGNORANCE OF GOD IS
THE GREATEST EVIL AMONG MEN

(1) O men, whither are you being swept away? You are
drunk! You have drained to the last drop the unmixed drink
of the teaching of ignorance. You cannot carry it, but are
even now vomiting it. Quit your drinking; turn sober; look
upwards with the eyes of the heart, and if you cannot all do
so, at least let those who can. For this evil of ignorance floods
the whole earth; it corrupts the soul imprisoned in the body,
not permitting it to anchor in the harbours of safety. (2) Do
not let yourselves be swept along by the powerful tide, but
take advantage of the counter-current, those of you who are
able to reach the haven of safety, and cast anchor there, and
seek a guide to lead you by the hand to the gates of knowledge
[*gnosis*]. There is the shining light, pure from darkness; there
no one is drunk, but all are sober, looking up with the heart
to him who wills [thus] to be seen. For he cannot be heard,
nor spoken, nor seen by the eyes, but only with mind and
heart.

But first you must tear off from around you this tunic
which you wear—this fabric of ignorance, this support of
wickedness, this bondage of corruption, this cloak of dark-

ness, this living death, this sensate corpse, this tomb you carry around with you, this robber who dwells in your house, who by the things it loves hates you, and by what it hates is envious of you. (3) Such is the hateful tunic with which you have clothed yourself; it holds you down in a strangle-grip tight to itself, so that you may not look upwards and behold the beauty of the Truth and the Good that abides in it, and hate the evil of this thing, aware of its designs upon you. For it renders insensible what seem to be organs of sense [but are not really], having obstructed them with a mass of gross matter, and cramming them full of filthy pleasure, so that you can neither hear what you ought to hear, nor see what you ought to see.

4

Tractate XIII (Concerning Rebirth)

THE SECRET DISCOURSE ON THE
MOUNTAIN DELIVERED BY HERMES
TRISMEGISTUS TO HIS SON TAT CONCERN-
ING REBIRTH AND THE COMMAND TO
KEEP SILENCE

(1) When in the general discourses, my Father, you discussed deity, you expressed yourself enigmatically and darkly. You gave no revelation, merely stating that no one could be saved before rebirth. And as we descended from the mountain after your discussion with me, I begged to be taught the doctrine of rebirth since it was on this point alone of all doctrines that I was ignorant; and you said that you would transmit it to me " when you are ready to become a stranger to the world." I am prepared and have strengthened the understanding within me against the deceit of the world. You then supply what I am lacking by those means by which you said that you would transmit to me the process of rebirth, setting it before me in speech or in a secret way. I do not know, Trismegistus, from what womb or from what seed the Man was born.

(2) My child, the wisdom of the mind is in silence and the seed is the true good. . . . But who does the sowing, my Father? For I am completely perplexed. . . . The Will of God, my

child. . . . And of what sort is he who is born, my Father? For he cannot participate in the substance which is in me. . . . He who is born will be different, he will be the Son of God, the All in All, composed of all the Powers. . . . You tell me a riddle, my Father, and do not converse with me as a father to a son. . . . This sort of thing, my child, cannot be taught, but God recalls it to your memory when he wills.

(3) . . . You give me explanations, my Father, which are impossible and forced. That is why I wish to make a correct reply to these things: " I have been born as a son who is a stranger to his father's race." Do not begrudge me your guidance, my Father. I am your legitimate son. Explain to me the mode of rebirth. . . . What am I to say, my son? I can say nothing but this: seeing in myself an immaterial vision produced by the mercy of God, I went forth from myself into an immortal body and am not now what I was before, but have been born in the Mind. This thing cannot be taught nor can it be grasped by this element formed of matter which enables one to see in this world. That is why I have had no concern for my first composite [human] form. I no longer have colour or sense of touch or size; I am a stranger to all these things. Now you see me, my child, with your eyes, but you cannot understand what I am by staring at me with corporeal eyes and earthly vision. It is not with these eyes that I can be seen now, my child.

(4) . . . You have thrown me, my Father, into a great frenzy and delirium. For now I cannot see myself. . . . May you too, my child, go forth from yourself like those who are haunted by dreams in their sleep, but in your case without going to sleep. . . . Tell me also this: who is the author of rebirth? . . . The Son of God, the One Man, by the will of God.

(5) . . . Now at last, my Father, you have rendered me speechless. Having lost my former senses . . . yes, I see your size the same, my Father, along with your external shape! . . . And in that you are mistaken. For the mortal form changes daily since with time it increases and decreases, altering itself like a deceiver.

(6) . . . What then is true, Trismegistus? . . . That which is not polluted, my child, that which is unlimited, without colour, without shape, unchanging, naked, shining, that which can be grasped by you yourself, the unalterable Good, the Incorporeal. . . . I am truly mad, my Father. For when I thought that you had made me wise, the perception which I have of my thought was blocked up. . . . That you may expect, my child. [You can perceive with the senses] that which is carried upwards like fire and that which is carried downwards like earth and that which is wet like water and that which blows throughout the universe like air; but how can you perceive with the senses that which is not hard, that which is not wet, that which is not tightly bound, that which cannot be pierced, that which can be understood only by the effect of its power and activity, that which requires someone who can understand birth in God?

(7) . . . Am I then incapable of doing so, my Father? . . . By no means, my child. Draw it to yourself and it will come. Desire it and it will be. Abolish the senses of the body and the birth of deity will take place. Cleanse yourself from the irrational afflictions of matter. . . . Do I then have executioners within me, my Father? . . . Not a few, my child, indeed they are fearful and many. . . . I am unaware of them, my Father. . . . This ignorance, my child, is the first affliction; the second is grief, the third incontinence, the fourth lust, the fifth injustice, the sixth greed, the seventh deceit, the eighth envy, the ninth treachery, the tenth anger, the eleventh rashness, the twelfth evil. These afflictions are twelve in number. But under these there are many others, my child, which force the interior man to suffer because of the prison of the body by means of the senses. But these depart from him upon whom God has had mercy, though not all at once to be sure, and thus the mode and meaning of rebirth is established. (8) Now, my child, speak not and keep holy silence for thereby the mercy from God unto us will not cease. Now rejoice, my child, and be cleansed by the Powers of God that you may be joined to the Logos.

[1]* The knowledge of God has come to us. And with its coming, my child, ignorance has been driven out. [2] The knowledge of joy has come to us. At its arrival, my child, grief shall flee unto those who receive it with open hearts. (9) [3] The power which I name after joy is continence. O sweetest power! Let us receive it, my child, most gladly. See how it has displaced incontinence upon its arrival. [4] I now name the fourth power, steadfastness, that which opposes lust. [5] This next step, my child, is the seat of justice. For see how it has driven out injustice with no need of a trial. We have been justified, my child, now that injustice has left. [6] I name for us the sixth power, that which opposes greed, namely, fellowship. [7] Now that greed has departed I go on to name truth and deceit flees; truth is at hand. [8] See how good has been fulfilled now that truth is at hand. For envy has left us; good has followed upon truth along with [9] life and [10] light; and no affliction of darkness has continued to come upon us, but all have been conquered and have flown off with a rushing noise. (10) You have learned, my child, the mode of rebirth. With the arrival of the Ten, my child, spiritual birth has been effected; it drives out the Twelve and we have been apotheosised by this birth. Whoever then has gained this godly birth according to mercy, has left behind corporeal perception, knows that he is composed of these Powers, and rejoices.

(11) ... Now that God has made me steadfast, my Father, I form mental images not through the sight of the eyes but through the spiritual activity granted me by the Powers. I am in the heaven, in the earth, in the water, in the air. I am in animals, in plants. I am in the belly, before the belly, after the belly, everywhere. Yet tell me also this: how are the afflictions of darkness (which are twelve in number) driven out by the ten Powers? In what way is this accomplished, Trismegistus? (12) ... This tent, my child, from which we went forth was constructed out of the circle of the zodiac and this in turn is

---

* The ten numbers which follow in square parentheses have been added by the translator and indicate the stages of the ascent of the soul.

made up of elements, twelve in number, of one nature, with a form that can take any shape in order to deceive man. There are pairs among them, my child, united in action. . . . Rashness is inseparable from wrath; they are even incapable of being distinguished. It is natural then and in accordance with sound reason that the afflictions of darkness should retreat as they are driven by the ten Powers, that is, by the Ten. For the Ten, my child, is the generator of souls. And life and light are united where the number of the Unit, that is, of the Spirit, is born. The Unit then according to reason contains the Ten, and the Ten contains the Unit. (13) . . . Father, I see the All and I see myself in the Mind. . . . This is rebirth, my child: to form mental images no longer in the shape of three-dimensional corporeality . . . thanks to this discourse concerning rebirth for which I have written these memoranda in order that we may not discredit the All before the crowds, [but only divulge it] to them whom God himself chooses.

(14) Tell me, my Father: will this body which is composed of the Powers ever perish? . . . Hush! Utter not impossible things! For you will sin and the eye of your mind will be soiled with impiety. The perceptible body of nature is far removed from [the body which comes from] real birth. For the one is perishable, the other is not; the one is mortal, the other is not. Do you not know that you have been born a god and a son of the One just as I have been?

(15) . . . I should like, my Father, to hear the hymn of praise which you said that you heard from the Powers when you came to the Eight.* . . . Since Poimandres did reveal the Eight, my child, you do well in hastening to be rid of the tent. For you have been cleansed. Poimandres, the Mind of the Absolute Sovereignty,† did not transmit to me more than what has been written down; for he knew that I would be able to understand all things by myself and to hear what I wish and to see everything; and he left it to me to do what is noble. Wherefore the Powers that are in me sing also through-

* Cf. 1. 26.   † Cf. 1. 2.

out everything. . . . I desire to hear, my Father, and wish to understand these things.

(16) . . . Be silent then, my child, and listen now to the fitting song of praise, the hymn of rebirth; I decided not to utter it with so little restraint except to you at the end of the whole discourse. It follows that this hymn cannot be taught, but is hidden in silence. So then, my child, stand in an open place, face the south wind as the falling sun sinks, and worship. Do the same also facing the east wind when the sun rises. Be silent, my child.

(17) Let universal nature hearken to the sound of the hymn!
   Be opened, O Earth, be opened to me, every bar of the
      abyss;
   O trees, wave not your boughs;
   I am about to praise the Lord of Creation,
   Who is both the All and the One.

   Be opened, O heavens, and O winds, be still;
   Let the eternal sphere of God hearken to my word!
   I am about to praise him who created all things;
   Who set the earth firm, and hung the heaven about it;
   Who commanded sweet water to flow from the Ocean
      into all lands,
   Both inhabited and uninhabited,
   To sustain and to create the whole race of men;
   Who commanded that fire should appear,
   For every use by gods and men.

   Let us all with one accord give praise to him,
   Who dwells on high above the heavens, the creator of all
      nature.
   He it is who is the eye of the mind;
   May he accept the praise sung by my Powers!
(18) Ye Powers that are within me, praise ye the One and the
      All;
   Chant in unison with my will, all ye Powers that are
      within me.

Holy Knowledge, I am enlightened by thee;
Through thee I sing praise to the intellectual Light
And rejoice in the joy of the mind.

Rejoice with me, all ye Powers,
And thou, O Continence, sing praise;
And thou, my Justice, praise thou the Just One through
    me;
And thou, my Spirit of Fellowship, praise thou the All
    through me;
O Truth, sing praise to Truth.
O Good, sing praise to Good;
O life and Light, from you comes the song of praise,
And unto you it returns.

I thank thee, O Father, the energy of my Powers;
I thank thee, O God, the Power of my energies.
Thy Logos through me sings thy praise;
Through me accept the all through the Logos, a spiritual
    sacrifice.

(19) These things the Powers within me cry aloud;
They praise the All, they accomplish thy will.
For thy will comes from thee and returns to thee, the All.
Accept from all a spiritual sacrifice.
Save, O Life, the All which is in us!
Illumine it, O Light!
Inspire it, O God!
For Mind is the shepherd of thy Logos.
O Spirit-bearer, Creator, thou art God!

(20) These things thy Man cries aloud,
Through the fire,
Through the air,
Through the earth,
Through the water,
Through the wind,
Through thy creatures.
From thee I have received the praise of the Aeon,

And, which is what I seek, by thy will I have found rest. By thy will I have seen this hymn of praise uttered.

(21) . . . My Father, I have set it also in my world. . . . Say " in the intelligible world," my child. . . . In the intelligible world, my Father. I have the power. My mind has been enlightened by your hymn and by your song of praise. I too have a very great desire to offer praise to God from my own intellect. . . . My child, do it not heedlessly. . . . My Father, I speak what I contemplate in my mind. I Tat offer to thee, my God, creator of generation, spiritual sacrifices. God, thou my Father, thou the Lord, thou the Mind, receive the spiritual sacrifices which you desire from me. For all is accomplished by thy will.

. . . Thou, my child, offer an acceptable sacrifice to God, the Father of all things. But also add, my child, " through the Logos." (22) . . . I thank thee, Father, that thou gavest me thy approval when I prayed. . . . I am glad, my child, that you have gained good fruits from the truth, immortal produce. And now that you have learned this from me, promise to keep silence concerning this miraculous power; reveal the doctrine of rebirth, my child, to no one so that we may not be numbered among those who discredit it. For each of us has been sufficiently occupied, I in speaking, you in listening. Now you know yourself and our Father through the Mind.

PART VII

PAGAN OPPOSITION
TO GNOSTIC THOUGHT

Gnostic ideas were militantly combated not only by the Church Fathers (examples from Irenaeus are to be found in Section I) and by Jewish rabbis, but also by some of the leaders of Greek philosophical thought. For our final section we therefore provide two examples, the first from the great Neoplatonist Plotinus (A.D. 204-270), the second from his disciple Porphyry (A.D. 234-301/5). At least Porphyry was vigorously opposed to Christianity as well as to Gnosticism, as was the earlier Middle Platonist Celsus (see Part III 1a).

The translation of Plotinus, ' Enneads,' ii. 9, is abridged from that made by Stephen Mackenna; see also C. Schmidt, ' Plotins Stellung zum Gnosticismus und kirchlicher Christentum ' (' Texte und Unter- suchungen,' XX 4, Leipzig, 1904); R. Harder, " Plotins Schrift gegen die Gnostiker," ' Die Antike,' V (1929), 53-84; id., ' Plotins Schriften,' III (Leipzig, 1936), 55-87; E. R. Dodds, ' The Greeks and the Irrational ' (Berkeley, 1951), 285-89.

The translation of Porphyry, ' Vita Plotini,' 16, is based on the text printed by J. Bidez and F. Cumont, 'Les mages hellénisés,' II (Paris, 1938), 249-50; cf. also R. Harder, ' Plotins Schriften,' V (Leipzig, 1937), 183. On the Apocalypse of Allogenes see H.-C. Puech, " Fragments retrouvés de l'Apocalypse d'Allogène," ' Mélanges Franz Cumont ' (Brussels, 1936), 935-62. An Apocalypse of Allogenes has turned up among the Nag-Hammadi books, as well as a book probably to be called Mesos and works ascribed both to Zoroaster and to Zostrianus.

I

Plotinus

(4) To those who assert that creation is the work of the Soul after the failing of its wings, we answer that no such disgrace could overtake the Soul of the All. If they tell us of its failing, they must tell us also what caused the fall. And when did it take place? If from eternity, then the Soul must be essentially a fallen thing: if at some one moment, why not before that? . . . Nor may we grant that this world is of unhappy origin because there are many jarring things in it. Such a judgment would rate it too high, treating it as the same with the Intelligible Realm and not merely its reflection. . . .

(5) Still more unreasonably: There are men, bound to human bodies and subject to desire, grief, anger, who think so generously of their own faculty that they declare themselves in contact with the Intelligible World, but deny that the sun possesses a similar faculty less subject to influence, to disorder, to change. . . . These teachers, in their contempt for this creation and this earth, proclaim that another earth has been made for them into which they are to enter when they depart.

(6) What are we to think of the new forms of being they introduce—their " Exiles " and " Impressions " and " Repentings "? It all comes to states of the Soul—" Repentance " when it has undergone a change of purpose; " Impressions " when it contemplates not the authentic existences but their

simulacra—there is nothing here but a jargon invented to make a case for their school: all this terminology is piled up only to conceal their debt to the ancient Greek philosophy which taught, clearly and without bombast, the ascent from the cave and the gradual advance of souls to a truer and truer vision. For, in sum, a part of their doctrine comes from Plato; all the novelties through which they seek to establish a philosophy of their own have been picked up outside the truth. From Plato come their punishments, their rivers of the underworld and the changing from body to body; as for the plurality they assert in the Intellectual Realm—the Authentic Existent, the Intellectual-Principle, the Second Creator and the Soul—all this is taken over from the *Timaeus*. . . .

They introduce a medley of generation and destruction. . . . They cavil at the universe. . . . They make the Soul blameable for the association with the body. . . . They revile the Administrator of this All. . . . They ascribe to the Creator, identified with the Soul, the character and experiences appropriate to partial beings.

(10) One other tenet of theirs . . . surpasses all the rest in sheer folly, if that is the word. They first mention that the Soul and a certain " Wisdom " [*Sophia*] declined and entered this lower sphere—though they leave us in doubt of whether the movement originated in Soul or in this Sophia of theirs, or whether the two are the same to them—then they tell us that the other Souls came down in the descent and that these members of Sophia took to themselves bodies, human bodies, for example.

Yet in the same breath, that very Soul which was the occasion of descent to the others is declared not to have descended. " It knew no decline," but merely illuminated the darkness in such a way that an image of it was formed upon the Matter. Then, they shape an image of that image somewhere below—through the medium of Matter or of Materiality or whatever else of many names they choose to give it in their frequent change of terms, invented to darken their doctrine—and so they bring into being what they call the Creator or Demiurge, then this lower is severed from his Mother [Sophia] and becomes the author of the Kosmos down to the latest of the succession of images constituting it.

Such is the blasphemy of one of their writers.

2

Porphyry

In his [Plotinus's] time there existed many Christians including sectaries who had headed away from the ancient philosophy —such as Adelphius and Aquilinus,* who possessed innumerable writings of Alexander the Libyan and Demostratus and Lydus and also published Apocalypses of Zoroaster and Zostrianus and Nicotheus and Allogenes and Mesos and the like. They deceived many and were themselves deceived, as if Plato had not drawn near to the depths of the Intelligible Nature.

For this reason Plotinus himself provided many refutations in his classes and wrote a book which we have entitled *Against the Gnostics* [*Enn.* ii. 9], leaving the rest for us to criticise. So Amelius composed forty books against the *Book of Zostrianus*, while I Porphyry provided many refutations of the *Book of Zoroaster*. I demonstrated that it was a forgery and a modern work, made up by the founders of the sect so that it might be supposed that their own doctrines were those of the ancient Zoroaster.

* Aquilinus is known as a fellow-disciple of Porphyry; for further suppositions about him see Bidez-Cumont, *op. cit.,* II, 249n. 1.

GLOSSARY
BIBLIOGRAPHY
INDEX

Glossary

Achamoth. Late Hebrew form of the word for " wisdom," used by some Valentinians; see *Sophia.*

Adonaios. Hebrew " Lord " (*Adonai*) with a Greek ending (*-os*); one of the seven planetary angels.

Aeon. Originally " age," in the sense of a long period of time; then used of space, or the spiritual being governing a vast space either in the *Pleroma* (q.v.) above or here below.

Archon. Greek " ruler," a political title applied to the governor of an Aeon.

Authentia. The supreme power above; " absolute sovereignty."

Barbelo. The perfect power or seminal Thought (q.v.) of the Highest God; perhaps a corrupt form of the Coptic *belbile*, " seed " (F. C. Burkitt, *Church and Gnosis*, 54).

Baruch. The heavenly messenger in Justin's book *Baruch*; perhaps an equivalent of the secret Hebrew name of God, as in Irenaeus, *Adv. haer.* ii. 24. 2; I, 336 Harvey.

Demiurge. The creator and maker of this universe (cf. Plato, *Timaeus*); subordinate and or opposed to the Highest God.

Eight, or Ogdoad. The sphere beyond the *Seven,* or Hebdomad (q.v.).

Four, or Tetrad. A group of four primary Aeons or, sometimes, the four " great lights " with which the process of emanation began.

Iao. Hebrew name of God, applied to one of the planetary angels.

Ialdabaoth. Perversion of a Hebrew name of God, probably Yahweh Sabaoth, applied to the ignorant *Demiurge* (q.v.).

Imitation Spirit. According to the *Apocryphon of John* the power

243

in man which resists the divine spark; perhaps derived from the Jewish idea of the " evil impulse " found in every man.

Naas. Hebrew " serpent "; a power either aiding or opposing the Highest God.

Nine, or Ennead. In the *Apocryphon of John*, the sphere beyond the *Eight* (q.v.).

Pleroma. The totality of the (usually thirty) highest Aeons.

Prunicos. The name given *Sophia* (q.v.) by the Valentinians, according to Irenaeus and Origen; given Simon's *Thought* (q.v.), according to Epiphanius. In the *Apocryphon of John*, *prunicon* (neuter) is something in Sophia. In ordinary Greek the adjective means simply " bearing " or " carrying " and is used for porters.

Psychic. One of the three classes of men (material or earthly; psychic; spiritual); a man who possesses soul and free will but not spirit. Valentinians used the word of Catholic Christians.

Saclas. Sometimes chief of the angels hostile to the Highest God; the equivalent of Satan.

Seven, or Hebdomad. Sphere of this universe, including the orbits of the seven planets; or an equivalent in the spiritual world.

Sonship. In Basilides' system the three " sonships " correspond to the " twin intellects " of God plus the soul; cf. G. Quispel in *Eranos-Jahrbücher* 16 (1948), 97-112.

Sophia. Greek word for " wisdom," denoting the first female principle emanating either from the Highest God or from a succession of Aeons.

Spiritual. One of the three classes of men (cf. *Psychic*); a man who possesses Spirit and is therefore saved.

Syzygy. Either or both of a " couple " or " pair " of Aeons.

Thought. The female principle, sometimes identified with *Sophia* (q.v.); the first emanation from the Highest God.

General Bibliography

I. GNOSTICISM

A. SOURCES

A. Hilgenfeld, *Die Ketzergeschichte des Urchristenthums*, Leipzig, 1884.

W. Völker, *Quellen zur Geschichte der christlichen Gnosis*, Tübingen, 1932.

H.-C. Puech, " Les nouveaux écrits gnostiques," *Coptic Studies in Honour of Walter Ewing Crum*, Boston, 1951,pp. 91-154.

H.-C. Puech—G. Quispel, " Les écrits gnostiques du Codex Jung," *Vigiliae Christianae* 8, 1954, 1-51; " Le quatrième écrit du Codex Jung," *ibid.*, 9, 1955, 65-102.

W. Till, *Die gnostische Schriften des koptischen Papyrus Berolinensis 8502*, Berlin, 1955.

M. Malinine—H.-C. Puech—G. Quispel, *Evangelium Veritatis*, Zurich, 1956.

P. Labib, *Coptic Gnostic Papyri in the Coptic Museum of Old Cairo*, I, Cairo, 1956.

B. STUDIES

W. Bousset, *Hauptprobleme der Gnosis*, Göttingen, 1907.

H. Leisegang, *Die Gnosis*, Leipzig, 1924 (ed. 4, Stuttgart, 1955).

H. Jonas, *Gnosis und spätantiker Geist*, I, Göttingen, 1934

(review by A. D. Nock, *Gnomon* 12, 1936, 605-12);
II, 1, Göttingen, 1954 (reviews by A. D. Nock, *Gnomon*
28, 1956, 124-26; R. M. Grant, *Journal of Theological
Studies* N. S. 7, 1956, 308-13).

R. P. Casey, " The Study of Gnosticism," *Journal of Theological Studies* 36, 1935, 45-60.

S. Pétrement, *Le dualisme chez Platon, les gnostiques et les
manichéens*, Paris, 1947.

H.-C. Puech, *Le Manichéisme*, Paris, 1949.

M. P. Nilsson, *Geschichte der griechischen Religion*, II (Munich,
1950), pp. 556-96.

G. Quispel, *Gnosis als Weltreligion*, Zurich, 1951.

F. L. Cross (ed. and tr.) *The Jung Codex*, London, 1955.

R. McL. Wilson, *The Gnostic Problem*, London, 1958.

H. Jonas, *The Gnostic Religion*, Boston, 1958.

J. Doresse, *The Secret Books of The Egyptian Gnostics*, New York,
1960.

II. JUDAISM AND GNOSTICISM

H. Odeberg, *3 Enoch or the Hebrew Book of Enoch*, Cambridge,
1928.

G. Scholem, " Ueber eine Formel in den koptisch-gnostischen
Schriften und ihren jüdischen Ursprung," *Zeitschrift für
die neutestamenliche Wissenschaft* 30, 1931, 170-76.

H.-C. Puech, " Numénius d'Apamée," *Mélanges Bidez*, Brussels,
1934, pp. 745-78.

C. H. Dodd, *The Bible and the Greeks*, London, 1935.

J. Thomas, *Le mouvement baptiste en Palestine et Syrie*, Gembloux,
1935.

W. L. Knox, " The Divine Wisdom," *Journal of Theological
Studies*, 38, 1937, 230-37.

G. Scholem, *Major Trends in Jewish Mysticism*, New York,
1946.

E. Peterson, "La libération d'Adam de l'ananké," *Revue biblique*
55, 1948, 199-214.

H. J. Schoeps, *Theologie und Geschichte des Judenchristentums*, Tübingen, 1949 (review by R. Bultmann, *Gnomon* 26, 1954, 177-89).

H. J. Schoeps, *Aus frühchristlicher Zeit*, Tübingen, 1950.

G. Quispel, " Der gnostische Anthropos und die jüdische Tradition," *Eranos-Jahrbücher* 22, 1954, 195-234.

R. Marcus, " The Qumran Scrolls and Early Judaism," *Biblical Research*, I, 1956, 9-47.

H. J. Schoeps, *Urgemeinde—Judenchristentum—Gnosis*, Tübingen, 1956 (review by A. D. Nock, *Gnomon* 28, 1956, 621-23).

A. D. Nock, " A Coptic Library of Gnostic Writings," *Journal of Theological Studies*, N. S. 9, 1958, 314-24.

J. Daniélou, *Théologie du Judéo-Christianisme*, Paris, 1958.

K. Schubert, *The Dead Sea Community*. New York, 1959.

G. Scholem, *Jewish Gnosticism, Merkabah Mysticism, and Talmudic Tradition*, New York, 1960.

III. CHRISTIANITY AND GNOSTICISM

H. Schlier, *Religionsgeschichtliche Untersuchungen zu den Ignatius-briefen*, Giessen, 1929 (review by A. D. Nock, *Journal of Theological studies* 31, 1929-30, 310-13).

F. C. Burkitt, *Church and Gnosis*, Cambridge, 1932.

W. Bauer, *Rechtglaäbigkeit und Ketzerei im ältesten Christentum*, Tübingen, 1934.

E. Percy, *Untersuchungen über den Ursprung der johanneischen Theologie*, Lund, 1939.

H.-W. Bartsch, *Gnostisches Gut und Gemeindetradition bei Ignatius von Antiochien*, Gütersloh, 1940.

R. Bultmann, *Das Johannesevangelium*, Göttingen, 1941.

J. Dupont, *Gnosis*, Louvain, 1949 (review by R. Bultmann in *Journal of Theological Studies*, N. S. 3, 1952, 10-26).

W. Baumgartner, " Zur Mandäerfrage," *Hebrew Union College Annual*, 23, 1950-51, 41-71.

L. Bouyer, " Gnosis: le sens orthodoxe," *Journal of Theological Studies* N. S. 4, 1935, 188-203.

R. M. Grant, " The Earliest Christian Gnosticism," *Church History* 22, 1953, 81-97.

E. Molland, "The Heretics Combatted by Ignatius of Antioch," *Journal of Ecclesiastical History* 5 (1954), 1-6.

G. Quispel, " De Joodse achtergrond van de Logos-christologie," *Vox Theologica* 25 (1954), 48-55.

H. Schlier, " Das Denken der frühchristlichen Gnosis," *Neutestamentliche Studien für Rudolf Bultmann*, Berlin, 1954, pp. 67-82.

R. M. Grant, *Gnosticism and Early Christianity*, London, 1959.

E. Peterson, *Frühkirche, Judentum, und Gnosis*, Vienna, 1959.

R. M. Grant—D. N. Freedman—W. R. Schoedel, *The Secret Sayings of Jesus*, London, 1960.

W. C. van Unnik, *Newly Discovered Gnostic Writings*, London, 1960.

Index

3. FIGURES FROM GRAECO-ROMAN MYTHOLOGY

4. JEWISH AND CHRISTIAN PERSONS AND PLACES

5. SOME GNOSTIC THEMES

Asceticism encouraged, 32, 47, 113, 144; cf. eunuchs, 112, 139

Faith inferior to Gnosis, 175

Fornication condemned, 65 (67), 97; viewed as indifferent, 43

Grace emphasised, 15, 25, 38, 191-2

Life a dream, 153-4

Love superior to law, 38, 175-6

Magic employed, 25, 29-30, 34, 192

Marriage criticised, 32, 37, 81-2, 139 (?); upheld, 95-6

Morality regarded as conventional, 25, 29, 34, 37, 39-40; as essential, 82, 137-40, 143

Mosaic law attacked, 25, 34, 36, 39-40, 45-6, 57; upheld, 42; analysed, 184-90

"Nature" determines destiny, 31, 34, 65, 128, 133, 139-40, 178-9, 194, 202, 206-7

Promiscuity encouraged, 25, 34, 37-8, 43, 47-8

Repentence stressed, 157, 237

Rites employed, 191-4 (*cf.* 90-2)

Sin viewed as non-existent, 65; as universal, 136-7

Women transformed into men, 66, 196

6. CHRISTIAN WRITERS

Clement of Alexandria, 39-40, 43, 143-5, 201 n., 207-8

Epiphanius, 41, 43, 61, 184-90

Eusebius of Caesarea, 41, 42, 43

Eznik, 93, 101-4

Hippolytus, 35, 43, 93-100, 105-15, 125-34, 145, 204 n.

Ignatius of Antioch, 30, 166 n.; Pseudo-Ignatius, 43

Irenaeus, 21-38, 41-61, 123, 162-83, 191-4

Origen, 89-92, 195-207

Photius, 208

Pseudo-Tertullian, 60-1

7. SEMI-CHRISTIAN APOCRYPHAL LITERATURE

Apostles, Epistle of the, 28

Clementine Homilies, 25-8, 42

Enoch, Apocalypse of, 58, 85 n.

Isaiah, Ascension of, 28

John, Secret Book (Apocryphon) of, 69-85

Judas (Iscariot), Gospel of, 60

Mary (Magdalene), Gospel of, 63-8

Paul, Ascension of, 61

Peter, Acts of, 63; Kerygma (Preaching) of, 201

Philip, Gospel of, 17, 35

Thomas, Acts of, 116-22; Gospel of, 111

Truth, Gospel of, 146-61

8. NON-CHRISTIAN WRITERS AND WRITINGS

Aristotle, 138

Celsus, 89-90, 235

Cornutus, 99 n.

Epicurus, 140 n.

Heraclitus, 113

Hermetica, 209-33

Homer: Iliad, 106; Odyssey, 111, 127

Marcus Aurelius, 138 n.

Pherecydes, 139

Plato: Cratylus, 38; Phaedrus, 28, 36; Republic, 143; Timaeus, 238

Plotinus, 235-40

Porphyry, 235, 240

Stesichorus, 24, 28

9. MODERN SCHOLARS (APART FROM BIBLIOGRAPHY)

10. BIBLICAL PASSAGES: GNOSTIC CITATIONS OR ALLUSIONS